PRAISE FOR
The Spiritual Practice of Good Actions

"Greg Marcus takes the wisdom and insights of the traditional practice of Mussar and refines it for the contemporary American of any religious background."

> —Rabbi Ira F. Stone, Mussar Leadership Program

"Whether you're Reform, Orthodox, or non-conformidox, pause your soul searching for a second and pick up this book. Greg Marcus's fresh take on the ancient wisdom of Mussar might just be the spiritual alarm clock you need."

> —David Sax, author of *Save the Deli*

"Greg Marcus's book will be invaluable for those who are committed to personal growth and are seeking a framework to examine the inner life."

> —Rabbi Jill Hammer, director of spiritual education
> at the Academy for Jewish Religion
> and author of *Sisters at Sinai*

"Greg Marcus swings the door wide open to spiritual seekers of all backgrounds with this hospitable introduction to Mussar."

> —Rabbi David Jaffe, author of
> *Changing the World from the Inside Out*

"*The Spiritual Practice of Good Actions* is an incredibly practical book to walk an inner path of spirituality. Greg Marcus introduces Mussar to Jews and non-Jews alike as a way to look inside and find the inner 'Soul Traits' one by one."

> —Jeffrey M. Schwartz, MD,
> author of *You Are Not Your Brain*

"A wonderful book that is rich in insights and practical information about the crucial spiritual work of self-transformation…This is down-to-earth Mussar that will be useful for everyone."

—Rabbi Yoel Glick, author of
Walking the Path of the Jewish Mystic

"*The Spiritual Practice of Good Actions* should take its place on the bookshelf of all seekers who are interested in the joys and challenges of serious personal growth."

—Marilyn Paul, PhD, author of *It's Hard to
Make a Difference When You Can't Find Your Keys*

"With clear, charming, inspirational writing and thoughtful self-help assessments, this book can help change your life for the better."

—Scott Behson, PhD, bestselling author
of *The Working Dad's Survival Guide*

"A powerful and practical guide to making a bigger impact on the world by being a better person."

—Karin Hurt, author of *Winning Well*

"[*The Spiritual Practice of Good Actions*] combines all the elements of contemporary learning in one engaging flow—deep wisdom, sources that surprise and captivate, a strategic framework that empowers the learner to keep learning, personal experience wittily and honesty shared, and a blueprint of practice to bring it all to everyday life."

—Estee Solomon Gray, tech entrepreneur, Jewish
community leader, and co-creator of Limmud Bay Area

"To all those interested in becoming a better person and learning about Mussar, Greg Marcus's *The Spiritual Practice of Good Actions* is an excellent life-changer!"

—Ezra Barany, author of the international bestselling thriller series The Torah Codes

"The fundamental message of Marcus's book is that spiritual journeys are becoming increasingly mainstream and that they are accessible to anyone wanting to become more whole and holy...His enthusiasm will make the most skeptical reader give Mussar a try and the book's step-by-step instructions will make the path easier to follow."

—Edith Brotman, author of *Mussar Yoga*

"Greg Marcus's book provides personal development and practical spiritual teachings in an easily understandable manner applicable by anyone from any religious or spiritual background...A much-needed modern spiritual guide to ethical behavior."

—Nina Amir, Inspiration to Creation coach and bestselling author

THE SPIRITUAL PRACTICE OF GOOD ACTIONS

About the Author

Greg Marcus, PhD (San Francisco, CA) is a practitioner, facilitator, and innovator of American Mussar, a twenty-first-century spiritual practice for an authentic and meaningful life. He earned a BA in biology from Cornell University and a PhD in biology from MIT. Visit him online at americanmussar.com.

THE
SPIRITUAL
PRACTICE
OF
GOOD ACTIONS

FINDING BALANCE THROUGH
THE SOUL TRAITS OF MUSSAR

GREG MARCUS, PhD

Llewellyn Publications
Woodbury, Minnesota

FIRST EDITION
First Printing, 2016

Book design by Rebecca Zins
Cover design by Kevin R. Brown
Cover images: tree—iStockphoto.com/19575442/©Pingwin;
pattern—iStockphoto.com/53557060/©Slanapotam;
background—iStockphoto.com/76710783/©songphon
Interior images: tree—iStockphoto.com/19575442/©Pingwin; photo
on page 43 © Stephanie Brandt; illustrations by Llewellyn art department

Llewellyn Publications is a registered trademark of Llewellyn Worldwide Ltd.

Library of Congress Cataloging-in-Publication Data
Names: Marcus, Greg, 1966– author.
Title: The spiritual practice of good actions : finding balance through the
    soul traits of Mussar / Greg Marcus, PhD.
Description: FIRST EDITION. | Woodbury : Llewellyn Worldwide, Ltd, 2016. |
    Includes bibliographical references and index.
Identifiers: LCCN 2016018662 (print) | LCCN 2016026269 (ebook) | ISBN
    9780738748658 (paperback) | ISBN 9780738749877 (ebook)
Subjects: LCSH: Musar movement. | Jewish ethics. | Spiritual life—Judaism. |
    Conduct of life.
Classification: LCC BJ1285.5.M8 M37 2016 (print) | LCC BJ1285.5.M8 (ebook) |
    DDC 296.3/6—dc23
LC record available at https://lccn.loc.gov/2016018662

Llewellyn Publications
A Division of Llewellyn Worldwide Ltd.
2143 Wooddale Drive
Woodbury, MN 55125-2989

www.llewellyn.com
Printed in the United States of America

To my wife, Rachel

You are my everything

Contents

———◆———

Contents

Introduction

On May 5, 2013, my cousin Sandy Kaplan died at the age of eighty-two, surrounded by his wife and children. We all loved and admired Sandy—not because of his MIT degree or business accomplishments but because Sandy was a great person. There are three reasons I can point to. First of all, Sandy was always there. Whenever there was a wedding, funeral, bar mitzvah, or other family celebration, Sandy was present. In addition, Sandy never had a bad word to say about anyone. He always had a positive, kind disposition, even through life's difficult times. When I was a graduate student in Boston, Sandy invited me to his home for the holidays and had me sit next to him so I would feel welcome. He was a *mensch*—a Yiddish word meaning "a person of integrity and honor."

Would you like to be a person like Sandy, widely loved and surrounded by loved ones when you go? You can be. Each of us has what it takes to be a mensch, and the Jewish practice of Mussar can teach you how.

How Do You Want to Be Remembered?

When I was younger I wanted to be remembered as a great person—someone remembered for all kinds of notable accomplishments. When I was a scientist I wanted to win a Nobel Prize. When I was in the corporate world I wanted to be CEO and to found a company that would change the world. When I published my first book I wanted to be remembered as a best-selling author. Sure, it would be nice to sell a lot of copies of this book and to impact a lot of people, but that is outside of my control.

Fortunately for me, the degree to which I live a spiritual life is almost entirely under my control. Throughout this book I'll share with you how Mussar has helped me uncover my weaknesses and begin to address them. I may even occasionally admit that I have some strengths, although my inability to recognize my own strengths is itself a weakness I am working on—which brings me to the next question.

How Do You Want to Feel About Yourself?

Today I would like to be remembered as a good person when I die. I would also like to feel like a good person when I come to the end of my life. In fact, I would like to feel like a good person now. Recently, one of my Mussar study partners, a retired mediator, told me how he used to ask his clients, "Do you like yourself?" He explained to me that if someone doesn't like himself, it severely limits how much he can give of himself to others. So I asked myself the question, "Do I like myself?" Very quietly, I realized the answer was no. Two days later, as I was getting ready for bed, I was overcome with a feeling of peace and contentment. I said to myself, "You are a good guy. All in all, you really are a good guy." The feeling of grace lasted much of the next day. But the following night, I awoke at 2:20 AM with a start; I had been having a nightmare. I won't share all of it, but in the end I was being chased by something terrible. Just when I thought I had gotten away, it started moving at super speed and caught me. I woke up, and the feeling of *I am okay* was gone.

I still don't really like myself as much as I ought to. But those two days of feeling okay showed me that it is possible, and for the first time I understood my true spiritual curriculum: to learn to love myself. Now that is a mission I can get behind.

How I Got Here

My spiritual journey started about ten years ago at an unexpected time and place. At the time my focus was almost entirely secular. I had my dream job, and I thought I was living a dream life. I had a great wife and two young daughters, and I was working at a Silicon Valley company that was literally revolutionizing human genetics research.

At first, the fact that I was working ninety hours a week did not bother me, and I took pride in my toughness. But my devotion to the workplace left me vulnerable, and I came to a place where, despite my PhD from MIT, I felt worthless. I felt like a bad husband, a bad father, and a bad employee. I was like an eggshell with all of the egg sucked out: hollow, dark, and empty inside. It started at the apex of my career; I was marketing the flagship product and leading the team developing the fourth generation with the scope and features that everyone wanted. As luck would have it, this project was the first one with major technical hurdles and setbacks. We made our launch date because I was not going to let us fail. We worked every weekend and through almost every vacation for an entire year. We got to launch, we shipped the product, and it flopped. It flopped in every single customer's hands, and management blamed me.

A few weeks after launch, I was sitting in a meeting with the top company leadership. None of the VPs and directors would make eye contact with me. Someone very senior started peppering me with questions: how much until this, how long until that, how many of this? I fumbled with my spreadsheets and she asked, "Don't you know how important this is?"

I wiped my sweaty hands on my pants and said in a quiet voice, "Yes."

"Well, it is time to start acting like it."

I walked out of that room with my shoulders down and said to myself in the hall, "Wow, I have really let the company down. I was the person in charge. This happened on my watch."

The following week I was at the largest human genetics meeting of the year. I was in a room full of our best customers and prospects when our featured speaker presented the product in a very poor light. I spent the rest of that afternoon at our booth in the trade show hall explaining over and over again that things would be just fine because we would have fixes for all of the issues.

That night a bunch of us were walking to a bar to blow off some steam when my cell phone rang.

"Greg, it's Mom. Grandma died today."

I stood on the corner with an umbrella in one hand and my cell phone in the other watching my colleagues file into the bar. My mother said to me, "Surely you are not thinking of skipping the funeral."

She was right. I was on the verge of not going. I walked back to my hotel room and burst into tears, thinking how proud my grandmother had been of me. When the meeting was over, I flew directly to the funeral. They waited an extra day so I could make it.

A few weeks after the funeral I was still really down. Now it was Yom Kippur, the holiest day of the year for Jewish people. The key thing on Yom Kippur is that we fast from sundown to sundown, we don't go to work, and we spend the day in prayer and reflection. It was three in the afternoon, and I was sitting toward the back of the synagogue by myself. My head was back, and my eyes were closed. I was conserving my strength because I hadn't had any food or water since the night before.

At the front they were chanting from the Torah in Hebrew. I opened my eyes and looked down at the translation: "Don't turn to idols or make for yourselves molten gods." My immediate thought was, "Idol worship? That ancient statue-worshipping thing is no longer relevant in the modern world..." And then this phrase popped into my head. It was like a clear, quiet voice saying, "You need to do what is best for the company." My stomach clenched, and I started sweating.

We only used the phrase "do what is best for the company" to justify something that was unpopular, like a layoff, a canceled project, or asking someone to skip a vacation. I thought about the nature of the company, an amorphous entity with a brand logo. I thought to myself, "Doing what is best for the company is not the same as doing what is best. My God, have I turned my company into a false idol? I guess I can't really be a 'family first' person when I'm working ninety hours a week."

I realized that my priorities were upside down, and I decided right then and there that I had to stop doing what was best for the company and start putting people first. I needed to take care of myself, and I needed to take care of my family.

Within a year, I had cut my hours by a third without changing jobs. Not a single person at work noticed. In fact, my career was thriving because I was no longer strung out and exhausted.

My life at home became a joy. One afternoon I walked past the door of the living room and stopped to watch my preschool daughter play with a friend. The scene was different from the wild, rambunctious play that was the norm. They were sitting on the floor cross-legged, talking quietly to each other. I couldn't hear what they were saying but they were so intense and serious. My eyes teared up as I saw this part of her I had never seen before. I thought to myself, "If I hadn't been home, I would have missed this irreplaceable moment."

The Moment of Change

For years I looked back and wondered where those words that popped into my head came from. If you are of a certain spiritual bent, you may be thinking that those words came from God. The collective view of how God speaks to us has been influenced by the movie *The Ten Commandments*—a powerful, deep voice booming in a way that we can't deny. While that makes for good Hollywood, that is not how these things actually work.[1] Today I have no doubt that God spoke to me, but it certainly was not what I believed back then—and you don't need to believe it now to keep reading.

---

1   In the book of Kings, the prophet Elijah is told to go outside and stand before the Lord. "There was a great wind, and earthquake, and a fire, but God was not in any of these. God was present in a quiet, subdued voice" (1 Kings 19:11–13).

It doesn't matter whether it was actually a message from Divinity because, whatever the cause, that moment of quiet changed my life. I began to act differently, and because I was acting differently, I began to feel differently.

Spending less time working greatly improved my life, but it did not answer what inside me was driving me to work so much in the first place. I am a bit of a seeker, and I wanted answers to some of the bigger questions about myself and life in general. Unexpectedly, the answers came from Judaism.

Judaism, as I perceived it at the time, was largely focused on rituals and traditions. I had not yet been exposed to the richness of Jewish thought that has developed through debate and scholarship over the last few millennia. Sages and scholars puzzled over great philosophical questions and how Jewish values can be applied in everyday life to answer those questions. It was the practice of Mussar that brought it all together for me and helped me find the answers.

Learning About Mussar

I first learned about Mussar in a family-based education program at my synagogue. I was taken by its concept that small gradual changes in everyday life can make lasting changes to our inner world. I had taken a similar approach of small gradual change as I extricated myself from my workaholic lifestyle. I not only wanted to learn more, I also wanted to teach Mussar to others.

I started taking an online class called "Everyday Holiness," based on the book by my teacher Alan Morinis. A few months later I was teaching a class of my own creation to a dozen people at my synagogue. I was only going to teach five classes, but we all wanted more. I taught five more and then five more again. In creating the class, I drew on Alan's book as well as from some of the classic Mussar texts written over the last one thousand years. My experience working on Internet and software products led me to innovate, and I created several visual tools to help our collective Mussar journey. You'll see these graphics later in the book.

Introduction

What Is Mussar?

Believe it or not, there is a solid argument that the Jews invented self-help over one thousand years ago. At the time, the Rabbinic scholars were trying to understand why it is so hard to be good. The Ten Commandments and other Jewish teachings clearly spell out how we should act. Yet many of us, both now and then, violate either the letter or the spirit of these commandments quite regularly. One of the answers to this question was Mussar.

Mussar is a practice that gives concrete instructions and guidelines to help you live a meaningful and ethical life. The first known Mussar text is a chapter called "How a Person Ought to Behave in the World" in a book written in tenth-century Babylon.[2] The first Mussar book was *Duties of the Heart* by Rabbi Bachya ibn Paquda, which was written in eleventh-century Spain. Rabbi ibn Paquda clarified a central tenet of Mussar: following the spirit of the commandments is just as important as following the letter of the law. For example, he scorns a scholar who focuses on pointless intellectual exercises instead of working to become a better person,[3] and he praises a scholar who worked for twenty-five years refining his conduct.[4]

In the ensuing centuries, the Mussar literature grew as scholars contemplated how various character traits like humility, patience, anger, and jealousy contribute to a good life. Mussar became a widespread movement in Eastern Europe, starting in the early nineteenth century under the leadership of Rabbi Yisroel Salenter. Rabbi Salenter transformed Mussar from a solitary practice to something practiced in community. Throughout its history, Mussar masters have used real-world examples and described situations that are often as relevant today as they were hundreds and thousands of years ago. In short, the struggles of our soul have not changed.

The fact of the matter is that we all have issues, whatever our religion or level of spirituality. Mussar teaches how to find those things

---

2   Gaon, *The Book of Beliefs and Opinions*, 357–408.
3   ibn Paquda, *Duties of the Heart*, 1:23.
4   Ibid., 1:25.

inside that cause us to get in the same situation over and over again, and it provides guidance for how we can begin to make small changes in our lives to help bring healing to the soul through greater balance. Rabbi Elya Lopian (1876–1970) defined Mussar as "making the heart feel what the mind understands."[5] I love this definition because so often we know what we should be doing but just can't seem to make ourselves do it.

Mussar can be translated from Hebrew to mean "correction" or "instruction."[6] In modern Hebrew *Mussar* means "ethics." When we practice Mussar we are adjusting and correcting our soul—but we don't try to adjust the whole thing at once. Rather, we focus on specific parts of the soul called soul traits. You'll get a chance to learn about your soul and soul traits in the next chapter.

Real-World Spirituality

Compared to Mussar, Kabbalah is the more widely known branch of Jewish spirituality. Kabbalah is spiritual/mystical and focuses on the unseen forces in the universe. Mussar is spiritual/practical and focuses more on our inner world and how it affects the choices we make daily. I'll be the first to admit that I don't know a lot about either traditional or modern Kabbalah. I do know that there is significant overlap in the traditional Mussar and Kabbalistic literature. If you are currently a seeker who has explored Kabbalah, Mussar will comple-ment and enrich your understanding. If you find Kabbalah a bit too "out there," you will be able to relate to Mussar because it is a very grounded practice.

The great twentieth-century Mussar master Rabbi Shlomo Wolbe defined spirituality as building your interior world,[7] and Mussar is the process we use to build it. In Judaism we don't wake up, decide to be spiritual, and then book a retreat to a mountaintop for contemplation. Jewish spirituality is about doing the inner work to change our very

---

5 Morinis, *With Heart in Mind*, 6.

6 Morinis, *Everyday Holiness*, 8.

7 Morinis, *With Heart in Mind*, 13.

souls so that we become better at living in the real world. We are not expected to become great overnight, and we only strive to become a little better than we were the day before.

One of my teachers, Alan Morinis, writes that we each have our own unique spiritual curriculum, meaning that we each have our own path in life, with a unique set of challenges and opportunities. We are presented with the same test over and over again until we pass it.[8] For example, my trait of humility is out of balance; I have a tendency to be arrogant. My arrogance hurt my relationships with others, especially my coworkers, for years. Each chance I had to say something arrogant was a test, and until I learned to make room for other people's opinions and feelings, I was caught in this cycle of starting well on a job and then gradually losing support from my colleagues. When I started bringing my humility into balance, I started keeping my mouth shut—passing the test—and became easier to work with. As a result, I was spared a lot of unnecessary stress and conflict.

As this example also illustrates, Mussar teaches that actions count; in fact, *only* actions count. We all have good intentions, but more often than not our intentions don't translate into good actions. Mussar brings our actions and intentions into alignment with Jewish values. What are Jewish values? Rabbi Hillel summarized it best: "That which is hateful to you, don't do to another. The rest [of the Torah] is just detail."[9] Mussar offers key insights to help us understand why we sometimes do the right thing and sometimes not. Hillel was articulating the Jewish version of the Golden Rule, more commonly known as "do unto others as you would have them do unto you." Whether or not you are Jewish, it is hard to argue with the Golden Rule as a universal ethical principle. Mussar turns real-world situations into opportunities for spiritual growth, which in turn make the world a better place.

---

8   Morinis, *Everyday Holiness*, 3.
9   Talmud Shabbat 31a.

The Three Principles of American Mussar

American Mussar is a twenty-first-century adaptation of traditional Mussar practice to the needs of the modern American Jewish population. I often get asked why *American* Mussar. American Mussar offers a distinct perspective informed by an American Jewish experience. There are 5.7 million Jews in the United States, which is second only to Israel in terms of population, and while we are hardly monolithic, there are common threads. For example, much of the American Jewish experience involves overwork, unfortunately, and as I wrote earlier, American Mussar started as a class to use Mussar as a way to achieve work-life balance. While many people in the class were overworked parents in their forties, the material resonated with a much wider age range and demographic.

In the nineteenth century there were Mussar schools named for their city; each had a particular focus. I don't think people in one city felt excluded because another school was named for another city. In an analogous way, it is my hope that non-Americans do not feel excluded because I chose to honor the country of my birth. The United States was the first country to grant Jews citizenship since the Roman Empire in 212 CE.[10] In addition, Benjamin Franklin's method for cultivating thirteen virtues was a major influence on the Mussar movement in nineteenth-century Eastern Europe. Franklin's innovations to help him track and monitor his behavior were adopted by Rabbi Menachem Mendel Levin in his book *Cheshbon Ha'Nefesh (Accounting of the Soul)*, which was first published in 1808 in Ukraine[11] and remains one of the most influential Mussar books today. American Mussar offers a distinct perspective informed by an American Jewish experience, which resides within an ongoing conversation among world and generational communities that stretches back for millennia.

Moreover, while *The Spiritual Practice of Good Actions* is written for a wide Jewish audience, I don't want to exclude anyone who isn't Jewish. I do not use Hebrew terms, and the messages and methodology

---

10   Chyet, "The Political Rights of the Jews in the United States."
11   Afsai, "Benjamin Franklin, Mussar Maven."

for becoming a better person draw upon universal principles and are widely applicable. If you are among the large population of American Jews who do not attend synagogue, this is a great book for you. At the same time, if you practice any degree of Jewish observance, this book will appeal to you as a complement to what you are already doing. And if you are not Jewish, I think you will be able to relate to the lessons about character and the non-ritualistic and doctrinal aspects of Judaism emphasized here.

American Mussar is built on the following three principles:

1: Jewish Values Through Mindful Living

Values are demonstrated by our decisions, priorities, and actions. Jewish values encompass a tried and true set of standards for both personal conduct and how to treat others. Too often we can get caught up living from moment to moment, letting life run past us in a blur. American Mussar will teach you how to live mindfully, with a thoughtful, deliberate approach for engaging with life in a rich, balanced way.

2: Alternatives to "God Talk"

According to a 2013 Pew Research survey, 62 percent of American Jews think being Jewish is about culture and ancestry more than religion. And more than half of those who say that being Jewish is about religion don't think it is necessary to believe in God in order to be Jewish.[12] Many among these populations find talk of God uncomfortable and either stop listening or become hostile at notions like "God has a plan." Perhaps this comes, in part, from the strand of American culture that values individualism, free choice, and personal responsibility.

---

12   Pew Research Center, "A Portrait of Jewish Americans."

Many people, including rabbis, struggle with God. In fact, when I first started teaching my Mussar class, I was unsure that I needed to include God at all. At the time my rabbi asked me to keep an open mind, and I'll ask the same of you. Whatever your feelings are about Divinity, there is a place for you in American Mussar, and I offer alternative vocabulary such as "the common thread of humanity" or "something greater than ourselves."

3: No Hebrew (Except for the Word *Mussar*)

Hebrew is an amazing language for spiritual study, and many authors use transliteration to present Hebrew words to an English-speaking audience. By their actions, they are arguing that the preservation of the Hebrew is important, and by implication something critical is lost if you leave out the Hebrew entirely. For the purposes of this book, however, I disagree. Even if something is lost in translation, the most important ideas and concepts are retained.

Mussar is about starting from where you are and taking that next step. Far too many people are left behind if comfort with Hebrew words is a prerequisite. If you would like to go beyond the teachings of American Mussar to texts that do refer to the Hebrew terms, I provide a table in appendix II that references the traditional Hebrew terms for the soul traits. For now, don't worry about learning the Hebrew terms. If it becomes important down the road, you'll have an opportunity to learn what you need to know without any stress.

Practicing Mussar in Community

Mussar can be effectively practiced by the individual, and it also provides a framework to build community. Community is central to Judaism and used to be central in the United States. A strong community provides people who will have your back no matter what. They will watch the kids, lend you money, take care of you when you are sick, and be there for all the big milestones in your life. Where do you have that today?

Unfortunately, as Robert Putnam and other sociologists have documented, community has been in decline in the United States for decades.[13] So many of us are working so many hours that we have allowed our career and company to step into the gap to provide the illusion of community.[14] On some deep level we know it is not real, but we long for belonging, for having a place. We evolved as a community, and for most people isolation is a path to depression and madness.

So while Mussar can be effectively practiced as an individual, it also provides a framework to build community on two levels. The first community opportunity is to find a study partner who is practicing the soul traits on the same cycle as you are and with whom you can discuss the readings, practices, and your own journey. The second community opportunity is to join or form a Mussar group. In the nineteenth century Rabbi Yisroel Salanter pioneered the creation of Mussar groups to bring multiple perspectives and greater depth of practice to each soul trait. I welcome you to visit americanmussar.com to join our virtual community.

How to Use This Book

American Mussar, like all Mussar, is a practice that exercises our spiritual muscles. In Mussar we will isolate one set of spiritual muscles for two weeks and then move on to the next set. Each spiritual muscle group is called a soul trait, and our practice is about taking actions that bring each soul trait toward balance.

First, read chapters 1–4 and complete the self-evaluation on page 25 to create your own soul trait profile. Chapters 5–17 cover the thirteen soul traits that form the core of American Mussar. You may wish to read the book slowly, focusing on each soul trait one at a time as you practice it for two weeks. Alternatively, you could read the entire book in one sitting to see how all of the soul traits fit together, and then go back and reread each chapter again as part of your practice. When you

13   Putnam, *Bowling Alone*.
14   Marcus, *Busting Your Corporate Idol*, 128, 135–6.

get to chapter 5, if you are torn whether to start right away or wait until you finish the book, my recommendation is to start.

When you begin your practice, I suggest starting on a set day of the week. You will practice each soul trait for two weeks and then move on to the next soul trait. Each chapter will have specific teachings and exercises to help you bring that soul trait toward balance.

After twenty-six weeks you'll have covered all thirteen soul traits in the book. Then read the conclusion for steps to help support you as you continue your practice.

Now Go and Live

Mussar teaches that the goal of our life is not to attain tranquility but to actively and mindfully live our lives doing good things. At the same time, however, you are not expected to suddenly transform into a saint. In fact, you will never be a saint. Neither will I; neither will anyone. As humans, we have both the positive and negative within us. They will always be there, but they do not need to be a source of pain and frustration. The key is to begin the process of making adjustments.

Your life is a car driving at ninety miles an hour. The last thing you want to do is slam on the brakes, as you'll certainly spin out and end up facing a direction that you neither wanted nor intended. By slowly braking, however, you can slow down and gradually turn with safety and intentionality onto the proper path for your spiritual curriculum. American Mussar is like a calm and gentle GPS for the soul.

PART 1

A Glimpse of the Inner World

Mussar is a practice, a means to internalize Jewish values to live a more ethical, meaningful, and authentic life. It is experiential learning, as we focus on conducting ourselves according to the spirit of the teaching.

While most of this book is all about the practice of Mussar, we need to do some learning first. In the next four chapters I will introduce you to the basic concepts and vocabulary of American Mussar. We'll revisit these concepts throughout the book to deepen your understanding as your practice progresses. From there we'll move on to part 2, where you will begin working with each of the thirteen soul traits.

Chapter One

——◆——

Meet Your Soul

Growing up and through most of my adulthood, the soul wasn't something I thought about. In fact, when I first started practicing Mussar, I didn't understand that Mussar is, in essence, soul work. I was more drawn to the self-help/self-improvement benefits of the practice. Traditional Mussar masters emphasize that Mussar is about becoming holy and elevating ourselves in the eyes of God. While some teachers can be quite emphatic that Mussar is not about self-help, an argument about such distinctions is unnecessary for our practice. In fact, the Kotzker Rabbi (1787–1859) would probably agree. He said that being an exemplary person—a mensch—is a prerequisite to becoming holy.[15]

When we practice piano, we know that we are getting better over time. Is it important that we understand all of the changes taking place in the brain and body that result in muscle memory and improved performance? Not at all. All we need to know is that "practice makes perfect." Yet we are, in fact, making changes to the internal world of our brain and muscles.

———————

15   Morinis, *Everyday Holiness*, 15.

When I began practicing Mussar I was making changes to my soul and didn't know it. Because Mussar is a spiritual experience in a way that playing an instrument may not be, it is important somewhere along our journey to acknowledge that what we are changing is our soul. Spirituality is all about changing the inner world.

There are also many misconceptions about the soul that we have absorbed from American culture that we need to unlearn. For example, before I studied Mussar, I thought that the soul was a subset of who I was—the part that contained my essence that would be preserved (perhaps) after I am gone. And I thought of my soul as the best part of myself.

I was wrong. I do not have a soul, I *am* a soul.

Now I understand that the soul is not merely a kernel of ourselves that lives on after death or just a part of who we are. In reality, the soul is the opposite—a superset of everything in the internal world. This encompasses the conscious, the subconscious, our rational thinking mind, and our emotions. When we practice Mussar we are changing our soul. The soul is not easily changed, so we work on making one small change at a time. Every action we take leaves a small imprint on the soul, and thus, over time, the small changes add up to profound changes in who we are.

Hacking the Soul

Mussar is the process of making internal adjustments that strengthen our character to live according to the spirit of Jewish teachings. As I just explained, what we are adjusting is nothing less than the soul.

Jewish scholars have been studying the soul for thousands of years, and the soul defies a simple explanation. Traditional Mussar draws from this literature, which describes the three parts of the soul in great detail. This level of detail is unnecessary for American Mussar practice. We can swim on the surface, knowing that there is a greater depth to explore if we wish. All we need to know to begin American Mussar practice is this: Judaism teaches that the soul has many parts, and the soul is the summation of everything we are—our conscious and subconscious thoughts, as well as our feelings and emotions. Everything we have done, learned, or felt has left an impression on our soul, and every action we take is a reflection of the state of our soul. As you practice Mussar, you may come to experience yourself as a soul.

By changing our soul, we change ourselves in lasting and meaningful ways.

In the last fifty years psychologists have uncovered the relationships between our beliefs (the internal world) and our actions (the external world). I've summarized the findings in figure 1. In short, our beliefs and values influence our priorities, decisions, and actions. Our actions, in turn, influence our values and beliefs.

Figure 1: *Soul Traits and Behavior*

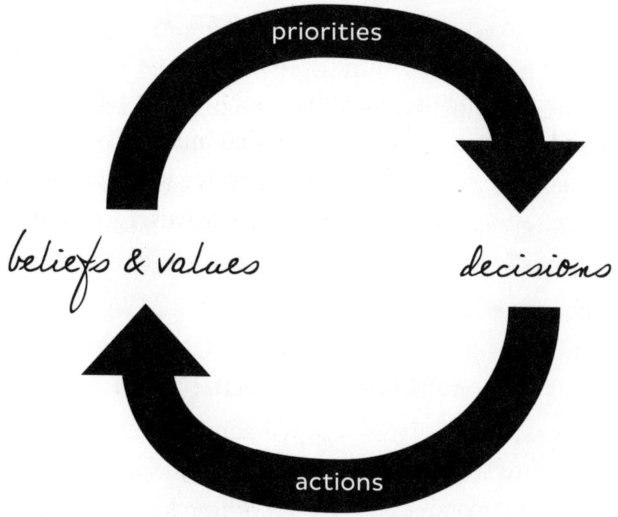

Take a look at this figure. It reminds us that our values are intimately linked with how we act every day. For values that are in a certain place, we will set our priorities according to those values. We make decisions based upon our priorities, and these decisions lead to action. With what we know of modern psychology and cognitive dissonance, our actions then go back and influence our values.

In summary, the soul is beyond any simple definition, yet we've learned that the soul influences our thoughts and feelings, and is ultimately responsible for our behavior. The spiritual paradigm of the soul influencing behavior, which in turn influences the soul, is paralleled by recent work in cognitive behavioral research. Mussar offers a unique way to both understand and influence the soul by focusing on soul traits, which are parts of the soul that we will study and experience in isolation.

The Soul Traits

One way to exercise is to isolate specific muscle groups. For example, one day you focus on the biceps; the next day you focus on the quads. Mussar is like extreme spiritual exercise, where you focus on a particular soul trait for two weeks and then move on to another. Soul traits are character traits—such as humility, patience, and order—that guide how we act and react in different life situations. Each of us has the same soul traits, but we have different amounts of each. For example, one person might be fastidious and another a slob because they have different levels of the trait of order. The soul trait of truth governs whether someone is truthful to a fault or constantly spins the facts to represent themselves in the best possible light. Having too much of a soul trait is just as bad as not having enough. The goal, then, is to bring each soul trait into balance, not to have as much or as little as possible.

To help illustrate this point throughout the book, I've created soul trait spectrum diagrams for each of the soul traits in Mussar. For example, figure 2 shows the soul trait spectrum diagram for patience.

Figure 2: *Soul Trait Spectrum for Patience*

angry frustrated | too little | *Patience* | too much | inactive fatalistic

You'll notice that both too much and too little patience have negative consequences. Too much patience leads to a failure to take action when action is called for. For example, someone with too much patience will stay in a bad job or a bad relationship too long, waiting for things to get better. Too little patience leads to impatience, stress, and/or irritability. We'll discuss patience in detail in chapter 6.

For each soul trait, we are somewhere along the spectrum from too much to too little. There are no right or wrong answers, and each of us will be completely different when it comes to the constellation of our soul traits. This should not surprise us, as we are all unique souls. In the next chapter you'll have an opportunity to look within and create a visual representation of the state of your soul.

Chapter Two

◆

A Soul Self-Evaluation

What makes you tick? What are the things inside that make you act the way you do? This is not an easy or comfortable question to answer. We are complex and have a lot inside that we may not like. The soul trait profile is a self-evaluation tool to make this task much easier. Before you begin, here are a few things to keep in mind:

- Don't take time to think or look up definitions of the soul traits. Answer according to your gut reaction.

- There are no right or wrong answers. I mean this literally, so do not spend more than a few seconds answering each question. The purpose of the exercise is to get you started looking within, not to capture an absolute truth or to make judgments. It is simply a way to create a baseline of capturing how you see yourself.

- Humans are notoriously bad at self-evaluation. For example, 93 percent of Americans think they are above-average drivers.[16] This, of course, is impossible: by definition, half the population drives below average. The upshot: don't worry about being accurate. Whether you spend two seconds or twenty minutes deciding the answer, you are unlikely to be objectively accurate. This is a first pass, and getting some surprises as you learn more is part of the process.

- You are the only one who will see this information. Whether you fill out the evaluation here or on americanmussar.com, your answers are private and anonymous.

Many people feel anxious about doing a self-evaluation. If you are one of them, take note of the anxiety and move on. One of your soul traits is being triggered. As you begin your practice, you'll begin to understand what is triggering you. For now, remember that you are safe and that however you are is how Divinity intended you to be. (Or, if you are unsure about Divinity, know that you are the product of what the universe made—your genes, your environment, your family, and your culture.)

You are unique and deserving of self-love just as you are, and Mussar gives you the opportunity to be the best version of yourself.

Soul Trait Profile Evaluation

Now it is time to take the evaluation. There is something powerful about seeing a graphic representation of your soul trait balance. It immediately jumps out at you that some areas are higher than others, and, as you'll see, the graph provides a means to track progress if you wish. While the individual spokes are not important in and of themselves, the effect of the graph is greater than the sum of its parts. It opens an emotional door to transformation—and frankly, it's kind of fun!

---

16 Svenson, "Are We All Less Risky and More Skillful Than Our Fellow Drivers?"

A Soul Self-Evaluation

On a scale of 1 to 10, rate yourself on the following thirteen soul traits. A 1 means that you have very little of that trait; 10 means that you have as much of that trait as you can imagine someone having.

For each soul trait, write in your score from 1–10, whole numbers only.

Humility: _____

Patience: _____

Enthusiasm: _____

Trust: _____

Loving-
Kindness: _____

Truth: _____

Honor: _____

Gratitude: _____

Order: _____

Silence: _____

Equanimity
(Calmness): _____

Fear: _____

Awe: _____

Now you can go the American Mussar website and generate a soul trait profile diagram for yourself: http://americanmussar.com/balance-look-like/. After entering your name and email address, you'll be prompted to enter a number for each soul trait before you are taken to a picture of your first soul trait profile.

The soul trait profile diagram is a spider graph, where each of the thirteen spokes on the graph represents a soul trait. One is in the center and ten is on the outer rim; the dashed circle is the halfway point. Each soul trait score is plotted on the spoke. We connect the dots to create the unique shape of your soul trait profile. Let's look at an example to understand what a soul trait profile does and does not tell us.

Figure 3: *Abe's Soul Trait Profile*

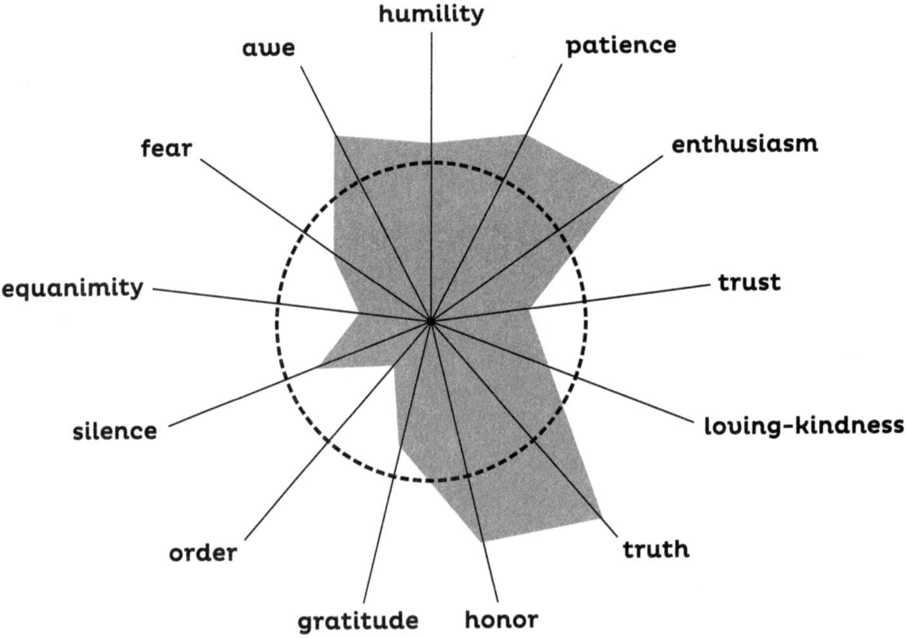

Our First Attempt Won't Be Accurate

Figure 3 shows the soul trait profile of someone we'll call "Abe." (Abe is a loose composite of who I was ten years ago and some of my former students.) Abe is a marketing manager in the biotech industry who recently cut his hours from ninety to sixty hours a week and is looking to Mussar to become more balanced in all aspects of his life. You will note that Abe rated himself high in certain traits like truth and patience, and has less of certain traits like trust and order.

When Abe showed his soul trait profile to his wife, he explained that the profile showed that he is a patient person.

"You aren't patient at all," she responded.

Abe was stunned—but we should not be since we understand that we are all biased when we look at ourselves.

Did Abe do something wrong? Absolutely not. The point of the soul trait profile is to begin the process of looking within. There are no right or wrong answers, and the conversation with his wife opened his eyes to look at himself in a different way. When Abe got to chapter 6 and learned more about patience, he adjusted his self-evaluation (figure 4). After two weeks of practicing patience, he went back again and did a third adjustment because he had become noticeably more patient (figure 5).

Figure 4: *Abe's First Adjusted Soul Trait Profile*

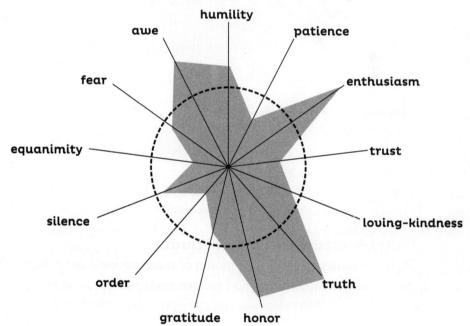

Figure 5: *Abe's Second Modified Soul Trait Profile*

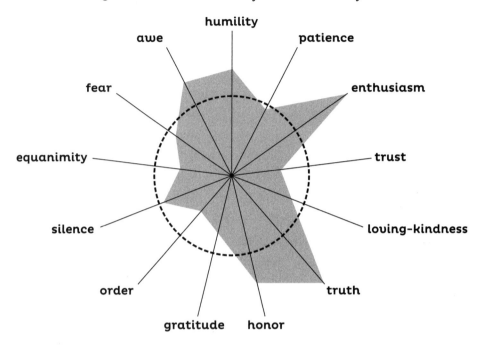

The Right Answer Is Balance

You probably noticed the dashed circle on each soul trait profile. The circle corresponds to a score of "5.5" for each soul trait, which is the optimum for perfect balance. The circle represents the soul trait profile of Divinity. Only Divinity is perfectly balanced across all soul traits. Whatever your feelings are about the existence or nature of Divinity, the point of balance sets the bar for our behavior. If you learn nothing else in this chapter, remember that having too much of a soul trait is just as bad as having too little. So whether we are inside or outside the circle for any given trait, our task is to inch our way toward balance in all of these attributes.

Figure 6: *Joyce's Soul Trait Profile*

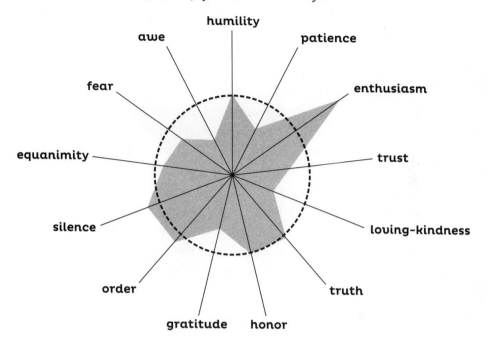

Don't Get Hung Up on Being Right

Joyce is a fictional person who is an amalgam of several people. She is a marketing director for a Silicon Valley company. She came to Mussar to find more balance in her life and to escape her feeling of constant stress. Joyce's initial soul trait profile diagram suggests that she is abundant in certain traits like enthusiasm and lower in certain traits like awe and kindness. (Joyce found awe particularly perplexing, since the soul traits were not defined before she was asked to fill out the self-evaluation.)

Although Joyce shares everything with her mother, she decided not to share her soul trait profile. In fact, Joyce was perplexed and angry at the thought of sharing her profile, anticipating that her mom would say that she was being too hard on herself. She thought, "Mom is clueless about who I really am." Maybe her mom is clueless because she never sees how Joyce shows up to people at work. Maybe Joyce *is* being too hard on herself. It doesn't matter, just as the exact number doesn't matter. In fact, it doesn't even matter if Joyce is "directionally right" about being below average in her initial assessment. The soul trait profile is only one stage in the process of looking within.

What does matter, however, is how much comes up for Joyce in this simple exercise. As she progresses in her Mussar practice, these issues and feelings will come up again and again, and she'll learn how to recognize the feelings and question where they are coming from. For example, her self-criticism suggests a humility imbalance, her anger toward her family suggests an honor imbalance, and her fear about taking the evaluation in the first place suggests a trust imbalance. Over time she will learn ways to bring the underlying imbalances back toward the middle, and her anger and pain will come into resolution.

For now, Joyce has gotten a snapshot of how she perceives her soul at the present time, which is a remarkable step forward. Before Joyce can begin her Mussar practice, though, it is important for her to understand more about the soul and how it can be influenced.

Chapter Three

◆

Four Assumptions About the Soul

There is an old but true joke: "Two Jews, three opinions." Passover, the most widely celebrated Jewish holiday, teaches one of the core and fundamental Jewish values: the power of asking questions. We question, we debate, we wrestle with issues, and we wrestle with God. When I was first exposed to the Talmud, a set of stories and commentary about the Torah, I was amazed to see that much of it was written as debate between rabbis, with the dissenting opinion given almost as much space as the prevailing opinion. The conversation literally has gone on for thousands of years, and it continues to this day.

The fundamentals of Mussar cannot be separated from Jewish values and teachings. Few of us have the time for an in-depth study of thousands of years of Jewish scholarship, so how then do we summarize Jewish teachings in a way that provides the necessary framework for American Mussar practice? We use assumptions.

In business, assumptions are a key part of the planning process. For example, to generate a five-year revenue forecast for a new product line, we make certain assumptions, such as how often a customer will want a new version of the product and how fast the overall market is growing. The assumptions may be right or wrong, but we acknowledge them as guideposts for our actions.

In a similar way, the following assumptions form the basis for your Mussar practice. Some of the concepts may be new to you, and a few may seem counterintuitive or even contrary to your current beliefs. I ask for your patience and an open mind. In each chapter we will revisit one of these assumptions as it pertains to the soul trait of the chapter; thus, over the course of the book, your understanding will grow. Remember that the rabbis and Jewish scholars have been studying and debating the nuance of these assumptions for thousands of years. There is much to understand and many layers you can explore if you wish in the years ahead. From a Mussar perspective, however, this type of book learning is only important inasmuch as it helps you refine your character and conduct in everyday life. For now, open your heart, assume that the following assumptions are valid, and see where that will take you.

Assumption 1: We All Share the Same Soul Traits and Have a Unique Measure of Each

"Soul trait" comes from the Hebrew word that is translated as "measure,"[17] which illustrates just how important it is that we remember we all have the capacity for balance in any of the soul traits. "Measure" reminds us that however much we have, we can add or subtract to change how we interface with the world. We all have the capacity to be outstanding people, and with work we can reach our potential.

The soul traits are a canvas we all share, and the amount of the soul trait is the color that paints the picture.

---

17 *Middot*, singular *middah*. Morinis, *Everyday Holiness*, 19.

Assumption 2: We All Carry a Divine Spark That Is Occluded By Our Baggage

We are made in God's image; this divine spark rests within every single person on this earth. If you are unsure about Divinity, you can think of this as a common thread of humanity or a core of goodness. As we go through life, painful things happen, and we gather "baggage." The baggage gets in the way of our divine spark, making it harder for us to be our best selves. Our baggage also makes it hard for us to see the divine spark in others, and our baggage makes it hard for others to see our own divine spark.

The divine spark is at the core of the soul.

Our task in Mussar is to allow the light of the spark to shine through. As we do our internal work, we can access this divine spark as a source of goodness and strength.

Even the most loathsome person you can imagine carries the divine spark. This is not an easy concept, yet it must color how we treat others and how we treat ourselves. This does not absolve people of accountability for their actions, and it does not mean that we should trust everyone we meet. But recognizing the divine spark automatically creates a mindset of respect and compassion.

Assumption 3: We All Have Free Will But It Is Not Always Accessible

Free will is a philosophical and spiritual concept that says we alone are responsible for our actions; we cannot be controlled by fate, God, or supernatural forces. We do, in fact, have free will, but do we always have free will?

Have you ever been out of control? I don't mean the alcohol-induced out-of-control feeling. We've all likely "lost it" more times than we care to admit. Your spouse does something that bothers you, and *bam*—regrettable words exit your mouth before you even know what you've said. Afterwards, you apologize and say, "I'm sorry; I was not thinking." It is true, you weren't thinking in those moments, which means that you did not have ready access to your free will.

This does not, however, absolve you of responsibility for the consequences of your actions. By analogy, a drunk driver who gets in a car accident and kills someone is still responsible in the eyes of the law because he took his first drink sober.

Mussar practice teaches us how to better access our free will and to strengthen our resistance against those reflex, emotional, or habit-driven behaviors that are unhealthy for ourselves and the people we care about. These automatic reactions are symptoms of an underlying spiritual imbalance. To quote Rabbi Yechiel Yitzchok Perr, Mussar helps give us more time by "opening the space between the match and fuse."[18]

Assumption 4: We Are Driven By a Conflict Between Good Inclination and Evil Inclination

Mussar teaches that within us there is a fundamental battle between the good inclination and the evil inclination[19]—think angel on one shoulder and devil on the other. This battle between the good and evil inclinations is so important that the remainder of this chapter explores it in more detail. These terms are translated from Hebrew, and while "evil" is not a perfect translation, it is the best one I have seen. This is not the kind of evil that we would associate with heinous acts. Rather, evil inclination refers to our base animal instincts, including the fight or flight response, our sexual instincts, and the gut reaction toward selfishness. The evil inclination encompasses those instincts we have that are critical for survival; it is only when they are unrestrained that they lead us into trouble. The good inclination, on the other hand, corresponds to our intellect and reasoning, as well as our social instincts to help other people.

The concept of a war within is hardly foreign to those of us who've grown up in the Western world. Psychologist Jonathan Haidt provides a modern example of the battle between different parts of our psyche.

---

18   Ibid., 59.
19   Stone, *A Responsible Life*, Kindle chapter 4, 928.

He describes human behavior using the metaphor of the elephant and the rider.[20] The rider is the intellect, and the elephant is our emotions. The rider can point the elephant in a certain direction, but if the elephant doesn't want to go, it takes a tremendous effort on the part of the rider to make the elephant go in a certain direction, which ultimately is a futile exercise. Haidt suggests ways to entice our emotions to change direction, which is the path toward lasting change.

My favorite illustration comes from a place where I learned much of my wisdom as a child—the original *Star Trek* series. In the episode called "The Enemy Within" a transporter accident splits Captain Kirk into the good Kirk and the evil Kirk. The evil Kirk gets into fights, swigs brandy from the bottle, and even tries to assault the beautiful yeoman Janis Rand. The good Kirk is kind and empathic, but he can no longer make decisions and thus has lost his ability to command. Spock says to McCoy, "And what is it that makes one man an exceptional leader? We see indications that it's his negative side which makes him strong; that his evil side, if you will, properly controlled and disciplined, is vital to his strength."

There is a story in the Talmud that follows a similar theme. The rabbis trapped the evil inclination and initially rejoiced. Soon, however, they noticed that no one did any work and the chickens stopped laying eggs.[21] Just as the rabbis needed to let the evil inclination free into the world once again, the two halves of Captain Kirk needed to be reunited.

The evil inclination is a fundamental part of who we are. Our challenge is to guide our evil inclination toward positive contributions. For example, ambition is good when it helps you achieve things in the world. Unbridled ambition, however, can lead to unethical and antisocial behavior.

---

20   Haidt, *The Happiness Hypothesis*, 4.

21   Yoma 69b. See also Genesis Rabbah 9:7.

The Talmud says, "The wicked—they are under control of their hearts. But the righteous—they have their hearts under their control."[22] Mussar teaches us how to keep our heart under control.

Whether the good inclination or the evil inclination is in control has a significant effect in daily life, as the Talmud teaches: "The righteous are swayed by their good inclination, the wicked are swayed by their evil inclination, and average people are swayed by both inclinations." Moreover, the sage Rava declared that "we are among the average."[23] If an exalted sage is average, then few indeed can reach the standards of being righteous.[24] The Bible says that "there is no righteous person in the [whole] land who will [always] do good and not sin."[25] In fact, no one can, for God created us with both inclinations.[26] Whatever your feelings about Divinity, the truth of the statement is self-evident from your own experience. Even the most praiseworthy people have flaws, which become evident as you get to know them better.

The four assumptions in this chapter will help you start your American Mussar practice without having to learn thousands of years of Jewish teachings. Depending on your background, some or all of these ideas may be new to you, and whatever your background, some of them may be uncomfortable. I ask you to trust the process. Try them out. Assume they are true, and see where that takes you.

Now it is time to transition from the theory to Mussar practice.

---

22 Babylonian Talmud Berakoth 61b. Bialik, *The Book of Legends (Sefer Ha-Aggadah)*, 547:111.

23 Babylonian Talmud: Tractate Berakoth 61b. Come-and-hear.com.

24 Babylonian Talmud: Tractate Berakoth 61b. Come-and-hear.com.

25 Kohelet 7:20, from Luzzatto, *Path of the Just*, 153. Except where otherwise noted, references are to this edition.

26 Babylonian Talmud: Tractate Berakoth 61a. Come-and-hear.com.

Chapter Four

◆

From Assumptions to Action

With his publication of *Duties of the Heart* circa 1040, Rabbi Bachya ibn Paquda wrote that it is not enough to be a Torah scholar; one must be "involved in both Torah [study] and acts of kindness."[27] He scorns a scholar who focuses on pointless intellectual exercises instead of working to become a better person,[28] and he praises a scholar who worked for twenty-five years refining his conduct.[29] I can imagine that his comments did not go down well in some quarters. Even today, in certain Jewish communities, it appears that Torah study and ritual observance are the highest priorities.

Following Rabbi Bachya's example, Mussar follows a different path. Mussar is a practice: actions we should take in everyday life to bring alignment with our aspirational values. By taking small, specific

---

27   Quoting the Talmud, Avodah Zarah 17b, ibn Paquda, *Duties of the Heart*, 1:35.
28   Ibid., 1:23.
29   Ibid., 1:25.

actions, we are making changes in the inner world—changes in our very soul.

I have seen people change and grow as they practice Mussar. Occasionally I see someone transform in a single class. The word *practice* is key. Judaism is a religion of deed, not creed. For example, Mussar teaches that it is not okay to hurt someone's feelings, even if we mean well. In other words, our good intentions do not excuse a bad outcome. In fact, the disparity between intentions and outcomes points to an opportunity for growth. As we adopt a more thoughtful and proactive way of living, we will avoid some of the stressful or awkward situations that result from ill-considered action.

American Mussar Practice Overview

Mussar practice has daily, weekly, and yearly cycles. The next part of the book has one chapter for each of thirteen soul traits. You will practice each trait for two weeks before moving on to the next one. At the end of twenty-six weeks, you'll go back to the first soul trait and begin the cycle again. Daily practice has three parts: meditation, mindful action, and journaling.

- To frame your thinking for the day, meditate in the morning for a few minutes on the given phrase associated with the particular soul trait you are working on. You can write on an index card to remind you of the mantra, then place it somewhere you will see it, such as near your bedside table.

- Mindful action throughout the day to learn how the soul trait is affecting your thoughts and actions.

- Write in your journal at night to capture the spiritual challenges of the day. Include both areas where you did well and examples of how you missed the mark. The writing is important, as it will make concrete the connection between your soul trait and the actions you take. Alternatively, use the journaling feature of the Pocket Mensch app to capture your observations as they are happening.

- Act in one or two small ways to modify your behavior toward balance. For example, if you are always the type who has to be heard in meetings, try to speak less. Conversely, if you are always afraid to talk during a meeting, ask a question.

By the end of each two-week cycle you will have a deeper understanding of where you sit on the continuum for that soul trait and what you need to do to move toward balance. It is not unusual to notice changes in yourself by the second week. By systematically going through each of the soul traits, you will discover soul trait imbalances that you didn't realize you had. In fact, being human means that we are out of balance on almost every trait. We are not expected to make great leaps and bounds but rather to change our lifetime of habits and thought patterns slowly. We need to make a series of small, step-by-step adjustments that will ultimately result in real, meaningful, and lasting changes.

Meditation and Mussar

Since Mussar is the process of building your interior world, we can only experience certain benefits when we learn to quiet the mind. We aim not to merely process information in head-space; we strive to make changes in our heart-space. One way to quiet the mind in order to open the heart is meditation. According to the modern mystic and meditation guru Rabbi Yoel Glick, meditation was once an integral part of Jewish practice that was largely lost millennia ago.[30]

As part of his work to revive Jewish meditation, Rabbi Glick has studied meditation with teachers from non-Jewish practices such as yoga, which has an unbroken meditative tradition that stretches back

---

30   Glick, *Living the Life of Jewish Meditation*, xxiii.

thousands of years. Rabbi Glick teaches that we too can benefit from techniques with origins outside the Jewish tradition to help us achieve the mental state ripe for spiritual growth. However, Jewish meditation offers its own set of chants, mantras, and visualizations to directly tie to our work of opening the heart to internalize Jewish values.

My first exposure to meditation came in a wonderful restorative yoga class where I learned to hold gentle, bolster-supported poses for up to twenty minutes. When I began practicing Mussar, my formal meditation started out very simply with two minutes each morning and gradually increased to five minutes. This simple practice helped me quiet the mind and was grounding as I worked on soul traits like patience.

Years later I discovered a set of guided meditations by Rabbi Yoel Glick[31] and my meditation jumped to forty minutes a day. At this level I experience a feeling that lasts throughout the day. Apparently, I am not alone in experiencing this. Scientific studies using MRI have shown that meditation brings brain changes that last throughout the day.[32]

If you are a more experienced meditator, I encourage you to try Jewish meditation.[33] There is a growing body of Jewish and Mussar-specific meditations that can directly support your journey to balance your soul traits.

If you are new to meditation, the thought of carving out thirty or more minutes a day to meditate may be daunting or discouraging. Don't worry: Mussar is about taking a series of small steps. I suggest starting with two minutes. Anyone can find two minutes. Make it part of your morning routine. Once you incorporate the two minutes a day, let go of worry about meditation and allow the practice to develop at its own pace. You may stay at two minutes forever or you may start meditating for longer chunks of time. Let go of any worry about the outcome. Just get started, and all will be well. In addition, look for an opportunity to

---

31 Glick, "Meditations By Teacher."
32 Pederson, "Meditation Shown to Alter Gray Matter in Brain."
33 Go to americanmussar.com/jewish-meditation for my latest suggestions on sources for Jewish meditation.

take yoga, tai chi, or other classes with a meditation component to help you learn how to let go for an extended period of time.

One of my first Mussar students, "Sarah," recently told me that she meditated for at least twenty minutes a day for over 700 days in a row. The streak started only a few months into her Mussar practice. This high-powered professional set a goal of fifty days in a row when she turned fifty. When she reached fifty it became 100; at 100 it became 200, then a year, then 500 days. When life got in the way and she finally missed a day, she said that she felt no sense of loss or sadness, which she attributes to the profound change in her that Mussar and meditation helped bring about. No one does something for 700 days in a row without feeling a benefit. Sarah's daily meditation made it easier to get into the zone at work, cope with difficult people, and appreciate events in a new way. She also experienced some deeper benefits, like a time in a business meeting when she was overcome by a feeling of love for everyone in the room.

Finally, remember that meditation is a skill, something that improves with practice. Once you get started, you will get better at it.

The Benefits of Journaling

Writing in a journal can be like kryptonite to some people. It is a hard habit to start, in part because it can be hard to confront some of the difficult things that happen during the day. I get it; I've been there. To be honest, I have no idea how I overcame my reluctance. I just followed the instructions in my first Mussar class and when they said to journal, I started to journal. I was also influenced by the growing body of scientific publications that show the benefits of keeping a gratitude journal. Dr. Robert Evans, professor at UC Davis, has studied gratitude for more than a decade. His work shows that people who keep a gratitude journal on a weekly basis feel better physically, are happier and more content emotionally, and feel more connected to others socially.[34] The purpose of a gratitude journal is to highlight the good things

34   Emmons, "Why Gratitude Is Good."

in our life, and it helps overcome the human tendency to take good things for granted. And when things go wrong, we have a tool to help us find the thread of good in whatever happens and to gain energy to move forward.

Mussar journaling is similar and goes a step further. A Mussar journal, like a gratitude journal, helps us notice what is going on inside. We use the journal as an explicit way to notice and adjust as we write daily. We also journal about a broader spectrum than just gratitude, changing our focus every two weeks as we change soul traits. As I write this, I recently finished two weeks on one of my more difficult soul traits, and I'm gleefully moving on to the next one. I've done some good work, and now I can work on something else.

Choice Points

Both meditation and journaling are important elements in increasing mindfulness to support the changes you are starting to make in your behavior. Behavior is the biggest indication of change and the driver of change in the soul. To understand how to act differently, there is one final concept that I must tell you about: the choice point. To understand the choice point, we must return to the subject of the good and evil inclinations that we started in the last chapter.

Rabbi Eliyahu Dessler, one of the foremost Mussar masters of the early twentieth century, describes the struggle between the good and evil inclinations as a battlefront. Behind the front lines, our actions are firmly entrenched such that we act without thinking to follow either the good or evil inclination. When we are at the boundary, however, we are faced with a choice and feel the pull toward both positive and negative behaviors. Rabbi Dessler called this a choice point.[35] For example, stopping at a red light under ordinary circumstances is in the category of an automatic behavior in the area of the good inclination. However, if we are running late, we may be tempted to race through the intersection while the light is changing. Choice points are critical,

---

35   Dessler, *Strive for Truth*, reprinted on Torah.org, accessed August 7, 2015, http://www.torah.org/features/spirfocus/FreeChoice-point2.html.

since that is where we have an opportunity to exercise free will and decide which way to go. We might make a decision to do right by our soul or to follow the evil inclination. It is only a choice point if the decision could go either way.

Figure 7: *Choice Points Only Exist Along the Muddy Boundary*

Photo ©Stephanie Brandt

To illustrate the metaphor of a battle between the good and evil inclinations, imagine that you are on a boat traveling toward the confluence of two rivers: one clear and one muddy. In some parts of our life we generally do the right thing and thus are sailing through the clear waters on the one side. In other areas, however, our weakness holds sway, and we are in the habit of following our base instincts in the cloudy waters to the other side.

In the middle there is a gray area where our spiritual challenges lie. The boundary is jagged, uneven, and in constant flux. There are places where the good juts out a bit or the evil inclination is starting to permeate under the good inclination. Each action we take influences our soul, making it more likely that we will make a similar decision in the future. Thus, when we follow the good inclination, the boundary is pushed to the right. When we follow the evil inclination, the boundary is pushed to the left. Dessler supports this conclusion by citing *Pirkei Avot (Ethics of the Fathers)*, which says "one sin leads to another," and the Talmud, which teaches "as soon as one has committed a sin twice, it is no longer a sin for him."[36] In America we call this phenomenon the slippery slope.

Rabbi Dessler teaches us that our choice points are a product of our education, environment, and state of spiritual development.[37] Two people with different spiritual curriculums will face very different choice points day to day. For example, let's compare the choice points between two men, one righteous and the other a thief. For the thief, the choice point is whether to take the television but leave behind the Blu-ray player. For him, that would represent a great step forward since he did not commit as big a crime as he usually would. The challenge for the righteous person is to give to charity with a feeling of loving-kindness instead of out of obligation.[38]

We all have issues. Mussar concerns the point of choice: that moment of conflict when we have to choose between being patient or yelling at the kids to hurry up and get out the door. Choice? When I start yelling it doesn't feel like a choice; it just comes out. While this is true, amazingly enough, two weeks after I began to focus on the soul trait of patience I experienced a dramatic change in my typical behavior. My kids were slow getting out the door in the morning, and I opened my mouth to yell at them. In that moment I recognized them as little divine souls just playing around and not giving a fig about getting to the car. I closed my mouth and smiled.

I have a student who went from being a hardcore, cut-you-off driver to someone who calls herself "the most polite driver in California" because she lets everyone go in front of her with a smile. As you begin

---

36   *Pirkei Avot* 4:2 and Talmud, Yoma 86b.

37   Dessler, *Strive for Truth*, 54–55.

38   Derived from an example from Rabbi E. E. Dessler shared by Morinis in *Everyday Holiness*, 23.

your Mussar practice in the subsequent chapters, trust the process. Meditate, journal, and take action. You may be amazed as you start to do things you never could have imagined.

PART 2

Balancing the Inner World

We are now moving on to the thirteen soul traits I have chosen to include in this book. Each chapter through the end of the book will begin with a short elaboration of one of the four Mussar assumptions that I shared in chapter 3. These discussions will help deepen your overall understanding of American Mussar practice and set the stage for the soul trait you are about to study. It may seem unusual to start a chapter without explaining the chapter's topic. The practice of Mussar is all about disrupting the normal way we do things in order to engage our emotions and bring about lasting changes into a new, more balanced normal. So if now or later you start to feel uncomfortable, that is okay: it is the evil inclination trying to hold you back. As you progress in

Mussar, you will learn to see such discomfort as merely a signpost on your journey and a great opportunity for growth.

Also, please keep in mind that each chapter is a means to help you build your personal practice. Each story and example is intended to give you perspective on how a given soul trait influences human behavior and thus provide a model of how to act. At the end of each chapter there is a section called "daily practice" with specific suggestions. To give you a quick preview, there are three parts to the daily practice:

- Each morning you'll begin by meditating on or chanting a short mantra to set the mental framework for your day.

- As you go through the day you'll observe how the soul trait is influencing your thoughts, feelings, and actions, and you'll make one or two very small changes in how you act to bring yourself toward balance.

- Each night you'll write down your observations in a journal to help capture and strengthen the changes in your soul.

Don't worry about the details of the practice for now. Instead, get ready to learn Mussar's surprising and countercultural definition of humility.

Occupy a rightful space, neither too much nor too little.[39]

Chapter Five

◆

Humility

I began my first humility practice with excitement and a bit of dread. Excitement because I was eager to start Mussar, and dread because I hated being called arrogant. (I guess I thought it was beneath me.) At the time I had no clue that Mussar teaches how humility in balance is the midpoint between self-effacement and arrogance. It took me a while to unlearn the Western definition of humility.

Assumption: We All Share the Same Soul Traits and Have a Unique Measure of Each

What does it mean for a soul trait to have a measure? Measure is a fundamental concept in Mussar, so much so that the Hebrew word for soul trait directly translates as measure. The question is not whether we have a particular soul trait; we do. The question is how much of that trait do we have?

There is a continuum from very little to an excess of a given soul trait. For each soul trait we sit somewhere along its continuum—we

---

39 Morinis, *Everyday Holiness*, 45.

may be closer to one side or the other, or reside near the middle. Our place along the continuum directly influences how we feel and how we act. The more we are out of balance, the more our actions tend to be hurtful or self-undermining. Our task, then, is to work in small, incremental ways to bring ourselves toward the point of balance.

This is not to say that we should have the same absolute amount of each soul trait. The medieval Mussar book *The Ways of the Tzaddikim* (*tzaddikim* translates from Hebrew as "righteous") explains that some traits should be exhibited often while others more sparingly. The anonymous author uses a cooking analogy to explain the point. Too little meat, "the dish will be thin...overgenerous with salt, it will be too salty to eat."[40] So, for a given soul trait (e.g., patience) the point of balance may not be the midpoint per se, and thus we wouldn't strive for equal amounts of patient and impatient behavior. (As an interesting side note, many speculate that the author of *Ways* was a woman, in part because it is unlikely that a man in the fifteenth century would use a cooking analogy.)[41]

You might be asking yourself how you will know if you are in a place of balance or if you have too much or too little of a particular soul trait. The answer isn't easy, as humans are notoriously bad at self-evaluation. The practice of Mussar helps us get to the answer by providing a wealth of stories, discussion, and specific examples to help set the bar for balanced behavior. First, we look to the Torah and stories for examples of how we should act with respect to the soul trait. Then we do practices—actual behavioral adjustments—which help us to both understand where we sit along the spectrum and to adjust our place toward balance. Now we will begin this process with a definition of the soul trait of humility.

---

40 *The Ways of the Tzaddikim*, 10.
41 Morinis, "The Middot Perspective."

What Is Humility?

Mussar teaches that humility is knowing your proper place in the world and acting accordingly. As a starting point for explanation, we need to let go of the American definition of humility, as it will bias our understanding of the Mussar-based humility practice. The traditional Western definition of being humble is to act in a non-boastful way. Some see humility as meekness and self-effacement, which they interpret as weakness.

Mussar also recognizes too little humility as arrogance and can be harsh in its condemnation of unbridled self-interest. However, the goal is not to be as humble as possible. Mussar teaches that humility in balance also recognizes that sometimes it is okay to be boastful or to project oneself into a situation. In fact, sometimes it is required. For example, Rabbi Yisroel Salanter said, "I have the mental capacity of a thousand men. Because of that, my obligation to serve God is that of a thousand men."[42]

Thus humility is defined in Mussar as knowing your right place in the world and not having too big a head (a trait that is shared with the Western concept of humility) but also not having too small a head. We should not be too self-important, and at the same time we cannot sell ourselves short. Sometimes we have more talent, more money, or better looks than others. It is okay to acknowledge such things, as long as we recognize that having "the goods" comes with the responsibility to use our powers for good.

---

42   Morinis, *Everyday Holiness*, 51.

Chapter 5

Spectrum of Humility

What happens if someone has too little humility? They become arrogant and self-important. You have probably encountered this type of boastful, self-important character. In their mind everything revolves around them, and were it not for their heroic presence in the world, all would be lost. One of the dangers of too little humility is disconnecting from other people. The more important we think ourselves to be, the less room we have to recognize the contributions or even the existence of other people. For example, when I was overworked in the corporate world, I thought the company could not survive without me, and it just wasn't true. I had an overinflated view of my own importance, which was disrespectful to the contributions made by many other people.

What happens if someone has too much humility? They become too self-effacing and may not take steps to stand up for themselves. I suspect you've met this kind of person too. They become the perpetual victim and never lack for a story of the latest injustice that has come their way. Being a victim is a convenient way to avoid responsibility and precludes the opportunity to take action to bring about change.

What do these two people—the arrogant one and the one with low self-worth—have in common? It's all about them. This gives us another clue about humility: it is about the relationship of self to others. When it becomes too much about "me," our humility is out of balance.

The Talmud teaches that "[a disciple of the sages] who possesses [haughtiness of spirit] deserves excommunication, and if he does not possess it he deserves excommunication."[43] How are we to interpret

---

43   Babylonian Talmud: Tractate Sotah Folio 5a.

this passage? Too much of an arrogant disposition is unbecoming for a rabbi, but too little would inhibit the rabbi's ability to exert his authority. Sometimes leadership requires us to make hard decisions, and humility in balance helps us step up to our responsibilities.

Moses and Humility

Judaism teaches that Moses was the greatest of the prophets because he led the Israelites out of slavery from Egypt and, more importantly, delivered the Torah from God. As the basis of Jewish law and values, the Torah is composed of the first five books of the Old Testament of the Bible, which are also known as the Five Books of Moses. Judaism teaches that Moses was the most humble of men; as it says in the Torah, "Moses was a very humble man, more so than any other man on earth."[44] When I first shared this lesson a student said to me, "That is ridiculous; Moses was hardly humble. He stood up to the pharaoh and led the Israelites out of slavery in Egypt."

This statement gives an opportunity to learn both about humility as well as the process of Mussar exploration. Judaism and Mussar encourage questions and exploration, but it is important to do so with an open mind. Every word of the Torah has been extensively discussed, explored, and argued.[45] As I explained earlier, multiple viewpoints are retained in the Talmud and other books of Jewish commentary. In this spirit, then, we are invited to join this living conversation.

It is one thing to say "I don't understand" or "I disagree"; it's entirely different to say "the sages were wrong." Even for the most learned rabbi, the bar to say the sages are flat-out wrong is very high. For those of us with a limited knowledge base, how could we possibly

---

44   Numbers 12:3. *JPS Hebrew-English Tanakh*, 310.

45   Orthodox Judaism teaches that the words of the Torah were literally written by God and cannot be wrong. Reform Judaism teaches that the words of the Torah were inspired by God but written by humans. The Conservative movement is somewhere in between. Those who are not sure about Divinity can view the Torah as collective wisdom that has endured for thousands of years of oral and written history because it contains lessons that still apply today.

know enough to dismiss a teaching as "ridiculous"? To do so could be evidence that we have too little humility. If you find yourself dismissing a teaching, ask yourself, "Am I really more knowledgeable?" Lessons from the sages are often counterintuitive and take some thought to fully understand. If the lessons were obvious, the sages would not be sages—merely smart people writing aphorisms for tea bags and fortune cookies! How much tea bag wisdom do we expect to survive for a thousand years?

In that spirit, let's return to the question of Moses. It is counterintuitive to think of the man who stood up to the pharaoh as the most humble man on earth. Let's assume for the sake of argument that the Torah is factually correct: that Moses was the most humble of men. In that case, either we do not know the story of Moses very well or we do not understand what humility is.

Moses was a man of great talents, and with those talents came big responsibilities. He stepped up and led the Israelites from slavery to freedom. At the same time, Moses never made it about himself. He did not wear fancy clothes or talk about his own greatness; he talked about the greatness of God. For example, when he went to the pharaoh, he said, "The Lord, the God of the Hebrews, has sent me to say to you: Let my people go."[46] If you are unsure of Divinity, focus on the key message that there is something bigger than ourselves and we are servants to the needs of greater humanity. In summary, Moses was the most humble of men because he stepped up to his monumental responsibilities and acted from a place of service, not ego.

A Modern-Day Moses

In December 1938 British banker Nicolas Winton canceled a ski vacation and flew to Czechoslovakia at the request of a friend to help deal with Jewish refugees. The Nazis had taken over the western part of the country, and the Jewish community was in terror from growing waves of anti-Semitic violence. Winton was not Jewish, yet with his

---

46   Exodus 7:16, *New International Version.*

two friends he set up a network that helped 669 children escape to Great Britain.

Winton's efforts were absolutely amazing. According to his *New York Times* obituary, his work "involved dangers, bribes, forgery, secret contacts with the Gestapo, nine railroad trains, an avalanche of paperwork and a lot of money. Nazi agents started following him."[47] When the British home office was slow in providing entry visas, Winton had them forged. His single-minded focus was saving the lives of the children, even allowing families with an avowed agenda of converting Jewish children to Christianity to sponsor and adopt the kids. Britain's Chief Rabbi, Joseph Hertz, was staunchly against allowing Jewish children to be adopted by these Christian families, even though to leave them behind meant certain death.[48] Perhaps Hertz was influenced by his evil inclination, which supplied rationalizations that the danger to the children wasn't that bad, and thus he stood by the empty justification of the need for cultural preservation.

Winton's actions would have gone unknown had his wife not found records in the attic fifty years later. Even then, he urged her to just throw them away. Here we have a man who risked his reputation, his money, his career, and his life to save Jewish children from a foreign country, and he never spoke of it for fifty years: a man of true humility indeed.

Bending the Rules

As Winton's example shows, sometimes humility requires that we bend the rules and travel outside of our comfort zone. There is a classic Mussar story about a man named Bar Kamza who tricked the Romans into thinking that the Jews were getting ready to revolt.[49] The Jewish leaders had the ability to disarm the plot, but it would have required

---

47 McFadden, "Nicholas Winton, Rescuer of 669 Children from Holocaust, Dies at 106."

48 Cesarani, "Nicholas Winton Saved Jewish Children, But He Also Has a Lesson for Our Current Migrant Crisis."

49 Morinis, *Everyday Holiness*, 48–49.

either killing Bar Kamza or violating the letter of the law about animal sacrifice. (Animal sacrifice was a big deal in those days.)

Rabbi Zechariah ben Avkulas argued that it would not be appropriate to either kill or violate the commandment, and thus Bar Kamza's scheme worked. As a result, the Romans destroyed the Second Temple, killed over one million Jews, and soon the Jews were exiled from the land of Israel for almost two thousand years.[50] Like Rabbi Hertz did almost two thousand years later, Rabbi Zechariah showed too much humility. He took the safe path of sticking with the rules when something much larger than the rules was at stake.

Franklin Roosevelt, on the other hand, was a leader who was not afraid to use his power to break the rules in order to help others, and in this sense he was humble in the model of Moses. He came to power in a time of national crisis and brought unprecedented changes to both the presidency and the role of government in the economy. As a result he brought hope and relief to millions of Americans, but he incurred the wrath of those who had prospered under the old system. In a famous campaign speech for re-election, he said,

> Never before in all our history have these forces [of the status quo] been so united against one candidate as they stand today. They are unanimous in their hate for me—and I welcome their hatred. I should like to have it said of my first administration that in it the forces of selfishness and of lust for power met their match. I should like to have it said of my second administration that in it these forces met their master.[51]

Who else but the president of the United States could have taken on such enemies? However, Roosevelt's humility also proved to be a weakness that led to the unraveling of much of what he accomplished. He went beyond simply wanting to do what was best and began to covet being the master. Roosevelt's desire to reshape the political landscape led him to try improperly packing the Supreme Court with allies, and then to campaign against anti–New Deal Democrats in the 1938

---

50   "Ancient Jewish History: The Great Revolt."
51   Roosevelt, "Address at Madison Square Garden."

congressional elections. Both of these efforts fed the perception (and perhaps reality) that he was trying to accumulate too much power for himself, and they led to huge losses for his party in the 1938 elections that effectively swept from office his allies and blocked his legislative agenda.[52]

Real-Life Humility in Practice

Fortunately, most of us will never be tested the way that Moses, Roosevelt, Winton, or Rabbi Hertz were. Yet how often do we do things a certain way because that is the way they have always been done? It is far easier to "go along to get along" than risk reproof or worse by sticking our necks out for something different.

One of my students returned to class and reported a career breakthrough after practicing humility for two weeks. He held a senior position in a start-up company but had a tendency to sit back and just let things unfold. He decided to occupy his proper space by speaking out more in meetings and was recognized by the CEO for his improved leadership.

Another student shared an amazing transformation in his personal life because he decided to occupy his proper space. He has two adult sons and up until that point had taken a very standoffish approach to their life choices. Then he realized, "Hey, I am their father, and it is my place to give them guidance on how to live." He called his older son, who was working in a solid job, and asked, "What is your long-term plan? Are you going to stay doing this low-level coding or do you want to make more of yourself?" The next day, his son sent an email saying that he had decided to apply to graduate school in the fall.

What a wonderfully inspiring story. The father has a long string of professional successes and did not hesitate to step into leadership roles at work. His humility practice led him to a breakthrough in how he related to his kids, in that he realized that he continued to have an important role to play in guiding his sons. As a parent, it is hard to

---

52   Busch, "The New Deal Comes to a Screeching Halt in 1938."

find that right balance between allowing the kids to make their own mistakes and being too pushy. Here, the answer was not in a book on parenting; it was within himself. He reflected on his proper space and, as a result, decided to take a small action with huge consequences.

Talent Leads to Self-Importance

"Wisdom is what brings a person to conceit and haughtiness more than anything else, because it derives from a noble quality that is inherent in the person himself—the intellect."[53] So wrote Rabbi Chaim Luzzatto in the early eighteenth century, and it remains true today.

Maybe the reason I didn't own a hat for many years was because my head kept getting bigger and bigger. I went to Cornell and MIT, and for a time had been successful at everything I'd ever done. There were also many times during my career when I got direct feedback that I came across as arrogant. For a while I didn't care, thinking that my contributions were so important and noteworthy that it didn't matter what people thought of me.

I needed advice from Rabbi Simcha Bunam, a Hasidic rabbi who lived in the late eighteenth and early nineteenth century. He told his students that they should keep a note in the right pocket that said *for my sake was the world created* and in the left pocket a note saying *I am but dust and ashes*.[54] When feeling down, take out the note from the right pocket. When feeling full of oneself, take out the note from the left. In those moments when I was too up or too down, the notes would have helped me get back toward balance.

For example, while I worked hard to get good grades, I did nothing to get my intellectual gifts. Those come from God (or the semi-random nature of the gene pool, if you are unsure of Divinity). Yes, I contributed to the success of the products I was managing, but my role was nowhere near as pivotal as I thought it was. Similarly, while I contributed to the big product flop that I shared earlier, I was merely the most

---

53 Luzzatto, *Path of the Just*, 153.
54 Buber, *Tales of the Hasidim*, 249–250. Quoted in Levin, "Dust and Ashes—and Holy."

visible fish in that poisonous pond. There was a corporate culture and executive team pushing to make the launch date no matter what.

Rabbi Luzzatto, whose quote began this section, went on to explain the danger of flattery to one's humility balance:

> Another deterrent to humility is keeping company with or being served by flatterers, who, to steal a person's heart with their flattery so that he will be of benefit to them, will praise and exalt him by magnifying to their very limits the virtues that he does possess and by attributing to him virtues that he does not possess, his attributes sometimes being the very opposite of those he is being praised for. And since, in the last analysis, a person's understanding is insubstantial and his nature weak, so that he is easily deceived (especially by something toward which his nature inclines), when he hears these words being uttered by someone he has faith in, they enter into him like poison and he falls into the net of pride and is broken.[55]

Does this not also ring true today? When we only hear praise, we can begin to believe our own press clippings. We ignore our faults and begin to think that we can't make mistakes.

Luzzatto goes on to offer a solution:

> A person's goal, then, is to seek honest friends, who will open his eyes to what he is blind to and rebuke him with love in order to rescue him from all evil. For what a man cannot see because of his natural blindness to his own faults, they will see and understand. They will caution him and he will be protected.[56]

---

55 Luzzatto, *Path of the Just*, chapter 23, http://www.shechem.org/torah/mesyesh/23.htm. For the same section with a slightly different translation, see the edition of *Path of the Just* translated by Yosef Liebler (Jerusalem: Feldheim, 2004), 166.

56 Luzzatto, *Path of the Just*, 167.

Chapter 5

Taking Your Proper Place

Where you stand is intricately linked to your level of humility. According to the Talmud, "Anyone who sets a particular place for himself to pray in the synagogue, the God of Abraham stands in his aid, and when he dies, people say of him, 'This was a humble person.'"[57]

Why is sitting in the same seat a measure of humility? By claiming your place, you give everyone else the freedom to pick where they sit. In addition, it reminds us that humility is not an attitude—it is reflected in how we act in the real world. Claiming a place is critically important. As the example below shows, where we physically locate is an indicator of where we sit on the humility spectrum.

One year on Rosh Hashanah I was part of a large group called to say the blessing before the Torah reading. By tradition, the person saying the blessing stands next to the chanter, which is considered a great honor. With a larger group, one would expect the group to stand right next to the chanter and spread outward. In this case, however, it was like an invisible force field preventing us from moving in close. Initially we were in a semicircle two to three feet from the Torah chanter. The rabbi and cantor motioned for us to move closer. We moved in but were not as close as we could have been. It was an uncomfortable irony that while it is an honor to be close to the Torah, somehow we all felt awkward and afraid that it wasn't our place to get so close.

Saying the blessing before the Torah is meant to be a joyous occasion of community, not a cause of fear. The rabbi, cantor, and the person chanting were all smiling and genuinely happy to have our participation. Because we were not enthusiastic, we lost an opportunity to make the most of the moment.

The following year I resolved to do better and mentally prepared to take my place next to the chanter. As I moved closer, I was paying attention to my interior world. I could sense something urging me not to "waltz up to the front." I recognized the voice as the evil inclination undermining my participation in a joyous event. I ignored the EI and

---

57   Talmud Brachot 6b.

tried to help my fellow board members with verbal coaching and a few gentle taps to bring them closer with me. One person I almost had to drag, and he uncomfortably stood behind me during the blessing.

In hindsight, I went beyond my proper place by dragging him with me. It was not okay to impose my Mussar journey on another. Put another way, my soul trait of honor was in play, in that I was not respecting his choice about where to stand. (More on honor in chapter 11.)

Know Your Place

In class we were reviewing the homework, writing "Not more than my space, no less than my place" on an index card to place by our bedsides. One of my students frowned.

"I don't like it. It seems like it is saying 'keep in your place.'"

For the student, the phrase brought forth hierarchical connotations. He shared that recently he had not been invited to a meeting at work that he thought he should attend. My answer:

"You are absolutely right. The mantra is telling you to keep in your place. The harder question to answer is *what is your proper place?*"

Have you ever felt bad because you were left out of something? When I was working ninety hours a week, I often felt upset when not invited to what I perceived as a "key meeting." Yet, at the same time, I complained that I had too much to do. As you can imagine, I was exhausted and strung out all the time—my need to feel important was overriding the importance of taking care of myself.

Work meetings can take on a distorted importance, where being seen and present becomes a source of external validation. If you are feeling hurt because you weren't invited to a work meeting, here are a few questions to ask yourself:

- How does my humility balance affect how I am feeling?

- Am I really so important that the business is better served by my presence in the meeting? Perhaps I can be more effective by getting my work done.

- Is it my place to decide who goes to the meeting?
  If it isn't my place, why am I taking this personally?

When you can accept that it isn't your call who goes to the meeting and that the business can survive without you, you will spare yourself a boatload of unnecessary pain. One way to overcome this issue is to practice trust in the Divine (chapter 8). You can trust that you will be okay and the business will be okay whether or not you go to the meeting.

However, it may be that the core fear is that you really aren't needed and are not important. While the outward actions of acceptance and focusing on the task at hand are similar, the purpose is different. Here you are working to decrease the hold work has on you in order to create space to allow self-love to grow.

Daily Practice

During the two-week cycle when we are studying a particular soul trait, there is a pattern we follow throughout the day.

Mantra

In the morning recite and meditate on a particular phrase that is relevant to the soul trait you are studying. The mantra for humility is "Occupy a rightful space, neither too much nor too little." Write this phrase on an index card or sticky note and place it by your bedside, on the bathroom mirror, or somewhere else where you will see it at the start of your day. Think about humility and the phrase *occupy a rightful space, neither too much nor too little* to frame your day. You may even want to create a little chant that you can say for a minute or two to reinforce the message in the depths of your being.

Observe

Where do you sit along the humility continuum? Are you too self-centered or too selfless? Here are some questions to help you decide.

- Do you feel stressed because you fear that you have spoken out of turn?

- Are you one of these people who leaves a meeting thinking, "I wish I would have said such and such. That person just walked all over me."

- Do you ever think, "They can't do this without me" or "How could they do this to me"?

The answers are clues to where you sit along the spectrum. As you go through the day, pay attention to the times when your humility is in play. Look for the choice points and the decisions that you make without thinking.

For example:

- Where do you sit or stand, in the front or the back?

- Do you feel superior or inferior to those around you?

- By your thoughts and actions, how often do you make it about you? For example, do you always jump in with your own example when someone is sharing a story?

- Do you rehearse past situations in your head, wishing you'd said something instead of staying silent? Sometimes, of course, it should be about us, but we step back when we need to step up.

- What do your clothes say about your humility?

Record your observations from the day each night in your journal. Your entry doesn't need to be long, and you do not need to write complete sentences; just a word or a phrase is fine. The journal is just for you; no one else will see it.

Journaling is an important step in the practice. By writing, we elevate our awareness and connect our conscious activity with the urges from the unconscious mind. And, most importantly, journaling leaves a trace on the soul.

Chapter 5

From My Journal

Great lunch with a friend today, and a few times I found myself holding back my comments to let him keep the floor, like when he mentioned the name of his soon-to-be ex-wife. She has the same name as of one of my ex-girlfriends and I could have shared a war story about how badly I was treated. Instead, I focused on listening and being there with him.

Act

Humility is the most fundamental soul trait. We will revisit humility throughout the book, and you will stumble across humility again and again in your Mussar practice. Because humility governs our interactions with other people, choice points present themselves regularly. As you start to record your observations in your journal, look for a small change you can make to bring your humility toward balance. Here are a few ideas that you can try as well. Don't try to do all of these; pick one or two to focus on. Record your intended practice in your journal.

- **Speak less when among people junior to you.** Rabbi Levin, the nineteenth-century Mussar master, counseled himself to remain silent in the company of men of lessor stature as a means to cultivate humility.[58] While twenty-first-century America does not have the explicit hierarchy of nineteenth-century Europe, implicit or explicit hierarchy remains a reality in many situations, such as the workplace or parent/child relationships. If you tend to be a blabbermouth, as I am, this also includes speaking less to give more space to others. Are you one of those people who just fills up a room? Try leaving more space for others.

- **Speak more if you tend to stay quiet.** Are you quiet when around people more senior to you? Do you play the role of junior partner in a friendship or romantic relationship? Look for opportunities to respectfully make your voice heard. Maybe

---

58   Levin, *Cheshbon HaNefesh (Accounting of the Soul)*, 147.

this is the time to ask for a raise or ask your secret crush on a date. These steps may be too big for you today; in that case, I encourage you to think smaller. For you, the right step may be to ask a question in a meeting. Whether you are speaking more or less, the key is to move beyond your comfort zone.

- **Change where you sit or how you dress.** If you sit in the front row or next to the leader, sit toward the back. If you try to blend in and not be noticed, sit closer or wear brighter clothes. Remember, you don't need to move from the front row to the back row. You could move halfway. How does it make you feel? Record your observations in your journal.

- **Engage in self-care.** In today's America, one-third of people describe themselves as chronically overworked and one-third are sleep deprived. Rabbi Hillel taught, "If I am not for myself, who will be for me?" How can you better take care of yourself? You are not immune to the health consequences of your life-style choices. This is a great opportunity to exercise more, go to bed earlier, or get off email earlier in the evening.

- **Park considerately.** You don't need to take up too much space.

- **Sing.** At a party in graduate school, someone from the UK said, "Let's sing!" There was a shocked silence, and someone whispered to him, "Americans don't sing." Since many people feel self-conscious about singing, especially singing with other people around, singing offers a great opportunity to practice humility.

    Rabbi Nachman of Breslov (1772–1822) said, "The most direct way to attach ourselves to God in this material world is through music and song. Even if you can't sing well, sing. Sing to yourself. Sing in the privacy of your home, but sing."[59]

---

[59] http://www.adolam.org/2011/09/rebbe-nachman-of-breslav-blasts-from-the-past.html.

If you are unsure of Divinity, think of singing as a way to attach yourself to something greater. Music has a way of hacking directly into the soul to reach the core of our being, so sing! Sing while alone in the car. Sing in the shower. Sing along with the national anthem. In your journal write about how you feel when singing.

The work you've done on humility has laid the groundwork for your entire Mussar practice. It will apply directly to the next soul trait, patience.

This too shall pass, and I have the strength to get by until it does.

Chapter Six

◆

Patience

I was looking forward to studying patience. I thought I was a patient person. Once I got into the practice, however, I realized just how impatient I was. In an ironic twist, I could not wait for the two weeks of practicing this soul trait to be over!

Assumption: We All Carry a Divine Spark That Is Occluded By Our Baggage

What does it mean for everyone to have a divine spark? We were created in God's image; as it says in the Torah, "When God created mankind, he made them in his own likeness. Creating them male and female, he blessed them and called them humans."[60] Rabbi Akiva taught it was an even greater blessing that we were told that we were made in God's image; as it says in the Talmud, "It is a sign of even greater love that it has been made known to them that they are called

_____

60   Genesis 1–2, International Standard Version.

children of God, as it is stated You are children of the Lord your God" (Deuteronomy 14:1)."[61]

By telling us, God is letting us know that we all carry a bit of the Divine within us and have the capacity for godly behavior. God is in perfect balance for all of the soul traits, which means that within us we have the capacity for balance too. If you are unsure about Divinity, you can think of this standard arising from the Ultimate, or Perfection. As humans we will never achieve perfect balance, yet this spark can guide us along the path.

In addition, think for a moment about your personal beliefs, values, and politics. Do you believe that every human life is sacred? Do you support programs to help the poor, and do you contribute to charity? Rabbi Arthur Green points out that these values are a direct outgrowth of the Jewish teaching that we are all created in God's image, and he maintains that this "Jewish soul" remain in Jews who may not "use the word God or soul in any other part of their vocabulary."[62]

"Baggage" refers to the painful things that have happened to us—scars from relationships, disappointments, and outright tragedy. Our baggage figuratively blocks the light from our divine spark and prevents us from being our best selves. Think of it as suitcases literally blocking your view of a lantern, or visualize an opaque window with cracks that let a little light through here and there. Or think of it as a windshield covered in bird poop; it is hard to see clearly through the poop! When we practice Mussar we are moving the bags, widening the cracks, and cleaning the windshield to let the light shine through.

Not only does our baggage block our own divine spark, it prevents us from seeing the spark in others. When we are feeling impatient because the person in front of us in line is taking forever to pay their bill, do we remember *their* divine spark? Often not—all kinds of names and judgments fill our head. When you start to remember the divine spark of the woman who can't find her checkbook, our need to get ahead of her takes on a new perspective. Surely our needs cannot be

---

61   *Pirkei Avot* 3:14.

62   Green, *Judaism's 10 Best Ideas*, 15–16.

more important than the needs of Divinity. Learning to appreciate the divine spark can be a key part in your patience practice.

Finally, one of the divine attributes is being "slow to anger."[63] The medieval commentator Rashi teaches that "slow to anger" means when we make a mistake, God is patient, hoping we will do better the next time.[64] When we are patient with other people, we too are slow to anger and thus are emulating this attribute, allowing our divine spark to connect with the divine spark in the people around us.

What Is Patience?

Mussar teaches that patience governs our ability to bear the burden of an uncomfortable situation. It is a gift from God, or, if you are unsure of the Divinity, a gift from the universe. It is the last resort given to us when things are outside of our control.[65] If we are stuck in traffic, we can throw some gas on the fire by getting upset, swearing, and honking the horn—or we can invoke our patience. The Hebrew word for patience derives from a word that means to carry a heavy load.[66] Patience, then, is bearing the burden of the situation until it is over.

Patience is the cure for helplessness. When we have no control of our choices and there is no action we can take to make things better, patience is what helps us get through. When my kids were mucking around when it was time to get out the door, becoming impatient and yelling at them did not get us out the door any more quickly. More often than not, in fact, it led to a temper tantrum that delayed us even further. As I brought my patience closer to balance, my children's behavior improved because my behavior improved. To be clear, they did not get out the door any faster, but we all remained calm, and sometimes I would even jump in and have fun with them.

---

63   Exodus 34:6, *Complete Jewish Bible*.

64   See Rashi's commentary on Exodus 34:6 on Chabbad.org, http://www.chabad.org/library/bible_cdo/aid/9895/jewish/ Chapter-34.htm#showrashi=true.

65   Morinis, *Everyday Holiness*, 57.

66   Vaeira, Bais Hamussar, 30 January 2012, http://baishamussar .blogspot.com/2012/01/310-vaeira.html.

In his classic Mussar book *Accounting of the Soul,* published in 1845, Rabbi M. M. Levin wrote,

> Woe to the pampered man who has never been trained to be patient. Either today or in the future, he is destined to sip from the cup of affliction…Moreover, he is beset with vain regret like those unfortunate bores who are full of meaningful remorse, making statements like, had I only not entered that business this would have never occurred.[67]

Notice how Rabbi Levin connects patience to humility. The pampered man has an inflated sense of self-importance, as if he could or should have been granted the power of prophesy to optimize the rest of the world to his benefit. Clearly, the same types of people lived in 1845 as we see in the world today.

Spectrum of Patience

Patient

angry
frustrated

too little

too much

inactive
fatalistic

Because I am in general an impatient person, when I started working on patience I thought that the goal was to become as patient as possible. Becoming more patient was the right answer for me in many circumstances, but for other people more patience would be exactly the wrong thing to do. Yes, it is possible to have too much patience. Too much patience leads to inaction and a fatalistic attitude. The overly patient person will stay in a bad job or a negative relationship, telling himself that things will get better. He thinks, "Maybe my boss will appreciate me more and will stop speaking rudely to me," or "My spouse's drinking will just go away, and the relationship will get better." Being too patient is about being passive.

---

67   Levin, *Cheshbon HaNefesh (Accounting of the Soul)*, 125.

Patience

When we have too little patience, we become angry and frustrated—impatient. When we become impatient, situations that already are not ideal get worse as we layer on an extra layer of emotion. Now instead of having one problem to deal with, like getting through traffic, we have two problems: getting through traffic *and* being stressed out and yelling at everyone.

Are You More Important?

When we are feeling impatient, it often involves another person. For example, you are impatient because the woman in front of you can't find the right credit card to pay the sales clerk. You are mad because you have better things to do than wait for her. You think, "Just use another card already." In reality, of course, she also has better things to do than search for the credit card. She got in line ahead of you fair and square, and you don't know anything about how she manages her finances. Is your desire to get out the door one minute faster more important than her desire to keep the accounting simple? Such a wait is a good opportunity to practice patience. Breathe in, hold, breathe out.

Romantic relationships also provide ample opportunities to practice patience. For example, one person is invariably slower, which can lead to the other person becoming impatient. How much of the impatience stems from hurt that the other person is not taking care of us in some way? Somewhere inside, the evil inclination is saying, "If he really cared, he would not be making me wait. He should be more considerate of my needs and my time." This reaction makes it about you and is an indication that the underlying issue is actually humility. How quickly your spouse gets ready is not a test of love. It has nothing to do with you and everything to do with their needs and the situation. Your desire not to wait is no more important than his desire to get ready at his own pace.

Remember the humility mantra from last chapter? "Occupy a rightful space, neither too much nor too little." To demand that a spouse get ready more quickly so that you don't have to wait, or to demand that the customer in front of you use a suboptimal credit card, are both examples of taking up too much space.

This is the first of many examples you'll see where the soul traits interact. Here, by practicing humility, we can actually bring our patience toward balance. Or, to put it another way, the impatience is a symptom of an underlying humility imbalance.

No Choice But Patience

As I explained at the beginning of the chapter, Mussar teaches that patience is a gift to allow us to get through difficult situations over which we have no control. Parenting teens is one of those situations. In her book *The Blessing of a B Minus*, psychologist and parent educator Wendy Mogel describes how hard it is for teens to establish their own identity. The rejection of and rebellion against their parents is necessary in order for them to work up the courage to leave the parents behind. And they need to learn by making mistakes.[68]

As painful as this can be for parents, Dr. Mogel explains that "shortcuts are not allowed."[69] She likens the teen journey to Israel's forty years in the desert. Although there was a direct route that could have taken the Israelites to the Promised Land more quickly, they needed the time to work through what is sometimes referred to as "the adolescence of the Jewish people."[70] In fact, when given the opportunity for the quick route, the Israelites reacted with fear and asked to go back to being slaves in Egypt.[71] They were not ready for the responsibilities of being a free people in their own land and needed forty years of making mistakes and gaining wisdom to grow up. In a similar way, teens need time to undergo the transformation from child to adult. But as a parent of teens, let me tell you that it is difficult to stand by and watch your kid make mistakes, and it is difficult to suffer through some of the normal rude teen behaviors. The only option is to be patient.

---

68   Mogel, *The Blessing of a B Minus*, 4.

69   Ibid.

70   Ibid, 3.

71   Numbers 14, 3–4.

A former student of mine was faced with a very different kind of situation that required patience: extended unemployment. This well-educated Silicon Valley professional had been unemployed for over a year and was stressed and unhappy that he couldn't find work. He explained how practicing the soul trait of patience made a huge difference in his life:

> When you are on a job search, you are constantly putting yourself out there, and you need to be patient because responses are slow and sometimes never come at all. The process gets harder and harder as the length of unemployment increases. I learned to recognize that I could not influence the outcome. Practicing patience helped me bear the waiting and focus my energy elsewhere. Instead of ruminating on why I had not heard back from someone or why I was unemployed, being patient allowed me to focus on the opportunity to use time in other ways. I started serious bike riding and made friends with other riders. In addition, I had the luxury to plan a wonderful vacation with my wife. If I had just been fixated on looking on job boards and waiting for email, I would not have had the mental bandwidth for these positive things.

While you may never be a parent or be faced with long-term unemployment, eventually you will be faced with a situation completely outside your control. Anyone who drives has been stuck in traffic, which provides a perfect opportunity to strengthen your patience muscles against the time when you'll really need them.

Patience or Action?

There are many times when patience can help us avoid unnecessary pain either to ourselves or to others. However, someone in a horrible job or an abusive relationship should not blindly wait for things to get better. They need to take action and be more proactive toward doing what is right for themselves or what is right in general. In the next chapter, enthusiasm, we will learn about when and how to take action.

Chapter 6

Daily Practice

Mantra

Write the following mantra on an index card, and place it by your bed or on the mirror in the bathroom where you will see it: "This too shall pass, and I have the strength to get by until it does."

Each morning, recite or chant the mantra to prime your brain to notice patience throughout the day.

Observe

Observe how patience comes into play as you live your life. Patience is about time perception. When we feel impatient time seems to crawl along; when we are patient time flows at its natural rate. When do you feel impatient? What are the triggers? What makes you acutely unhappy over the course of the day? Are you being too patient when, perhaps, action is called for?

When you find something that triggers you, write down what happened in your journal. You don't need to write down full sentences, and this isn't for anyone but you. After a few days, go back and read your entries. Do you see any patterns?

From My Journal

I had an interesting encounter with patience today. My girls were, as usual, taking a long time getting out the door, and my frustration was building. Then I suddenly remembered to look for their divine sparks. I started thinking of them as little girls who were not very old and mature. My anger instantly cooled and I was able to wait patiently for them to leave.

Once when I was practicing patience I had a very painful personal episode. It gave me a clear idea of what it means to bear the burden of the situation.

Here I was in my patience curriculum. I lost patience and raised my voice with one of the other volunteers on the committee because he tried to take over the meeting I was leading. Now the other volunteers do not want to serve on this committee with me. Is this an issue I brought on myself? Should I have just gone along? I did what I thought was right, but I also raised my voice out of impatience. A friend of mine noticed that I had raised my voice from the other room, so this must be true. I think the punishment to leave this committee is unfair, but with the others against me there could not be any other outcome. This is something I need to bear. I feel sad but not anxious. I guess the message is loud and clear: I need to work on patience.

Act

Delays become an opportunity to practice patience. It can be as simple as when you are stuck in a line; you can tell yourself, "This is a good opportunity to practice patience." Remember, if you are content in a given moment, you don't need patience. Patience is bearing the burden of something unpleasant. Here are some suggestions for ways to cultivate patience:

- **Remind yourself that it is okay to be patient because things will work out eventually.** When I do this, I just feel better. My mind opens, I begin to take deeper breaths, and my head clears of negative thoughts.

- **Give thanks for the opportunity to practice patience when you find yourself becoming impatient.** Dr. Wendy Mogel suggests the following prayer for parents tested by adolescents: "Thank you, God, for this test of my spiritual elevation."[72] We can use the same prayer in any situation that tests us.

- **Meditate on the mental image of a patient person.** Pick someone you know who is very patient, and meditate on this person's image. I picked my maternal grandfather, Philip Menchel. He graduated high school in 1932, right in the heart of the Great Depression. He was not able to go to college, but he never once complained to me about it. Grandpa Phil took it

---

72   Mogel, 4. If you are unsure about Divinity, use the word *universe* instead of God.

upon himself to learn and was incredibly widely read. Plus, he was just a kind and patient man.

- **Look for the divine spark in others.** For example, if you are waiting in a public place, instead of getting out your phone, look at the people around you. Watch their faces and look inside for their divine spark. Is it on the forehead or deep within their heart?

- **Speak more or less.** If you are at one of the patience extremes, you are likely speaking either too much or too little. Moderating when you speak is great practice for adjusting your patience balance. For example, if you are too patient, look for an opportunity to speak up at a time when you ordinarily may have remained silent.

- **Meditate.** By meditating at a time when you are not feeling impatient or stressed, you will have the ability to invoke a small moment of meditation in those times when you are feeling stressed.

- **Summon a song from your playlist.** Rabbi Nachman of Breslov (1772–1811) said, "Get into the habit of always singing a tune. It will give you a new life and send joy into your soul." Stuck in traffic? Sing along with the radio. Waiting in line? Hum a tune. Feeling stuck in a job or relationship? Put on some empowering music and sing along.

Make the most of each moment.

Chapter Seven
◆
Enthusiasm

I was looking forward to studying enthusiasm when I started the first time, and it remains one of my favorite soul traits. Enthusiasm drives the energy to take action.

Assumption: We All Have Free Will But It Is Not Always Accessible

There are times when we know we should do something, but we just can't get up the energy to do it. It may be something small, like putting the dirty glass in the dishwasher instead of on the counter. Or it could be something larger, like getting out of bed in the morning. Sometimes it is almost like we are fighting through molasses to get anything done. In theory, if we know the right thing to do, free will should just let us make the choice to do it. But sometimes it is hard to access the energy that we need in order to carry out the task. Other times, of course, our free will is much closer to the surface—for example, when rationalizations justify our failure to take action.

On the flip side, sometimes we are so enthusiastic—so jazzed about something—that we start doing it before we really think about the consequences. Here it is hard to be patient enough to think it through, and our energy carries us along to do something we know we'll regret.

Free will is about making an active choice. When our enthusiasm is out of balance, we are not taking advantage of this ability to choose.

What Is Enthusiasm?

Enthusiasm is the energy that drives us to action—but not just any action. Enthusiasm in balance is about applying our energy toward positive things to make the world a better place and to make ourselves better people. We don't want to go through life just checking boxes and accomplishing things in a half-assed way. The Talmud teaches that a good deed is only credited upon its completion.[73] Enthusiasm is called an ornament that perfects the other soul traits because it helps us complete the good deeds we start.[74] Rabbi Shlomo Wolbe taught that a good deed or commandment done late or done without enthusiasm is not one that *could* go wrong; it is one that has already gone wrong because we have not made the most of an opportunity to do good.[75] Rabbi Luzzatto warned that the evil inclination works not only to lure us to do the wrong thing; it also works to prevent us from doing the right thing.[76]

I am reminded of a teaching by the great Jewish sage Woody Allen, who said that "80 percent of life is showing up."[77] If Allen were actually a sage in the Talmud, there would be thousands of years of commentary on the statement, of which some would undoubtedly connect the teaching to the importance of being present and taking an action-oriented approach to life. Allen made the statement within the context of explaining that many people tell him they want to be a writer but never finish their first book or screenplay. He explains that people who

---

73   Genesis Rabbah 85:3.
74   Zaloshinsky, *The Ways of the Tzaddikim*, 287.
75   Morinis, *Everyday Holiness*, 127.
76   Luzzatto, *Path of the Just*, 37.
77   Safire, "On Language; The Elision Fields."

do complete the screenplay are more than halfway to something really good, like getting it produced.[78]

I must say, I find it super cool that a Woody Allen statement I've heard many times can be traced to a Jewish value; I don't think the connection is a coincidence. Allen, like many secular American Jews, has internalized Jewish values to a much larger degree than he realizes.

Spectrum of Enthusiasm

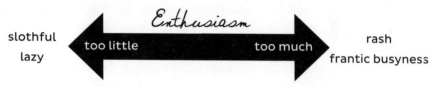

slothful
lazy

too little   too much

rash
frantic busyness

What happens if we have too much enthusiasm? We make rash decisions and get caught up in frenetic busyness. People with too much enthusiasm need to slow down and think about the consequences of their actions. Rabbi Luzzatto reminds us that frantically piling up tasks is one of the tricks that the evil inclination uses to prevent us from taking the time to reflect and consider the proper course of action.[79] It is not about just doing something, but doing the right thing. Our overall mission is to repair the world, which we are best situated to do when we embrace life with enthusiasm in balance.

Too little enthusiasm brings slothful laziness. I must say that I cringe when I read this. Lazy seems harsh and judgmental because I get that heavy molasses feeling from time to time. I need to do the dishes and I just cannot seem to get the energy to drag my butt off the couch to do it. Is laziness the right word to use? Sometimes.

---

78   Ibid.

79   Luzzatto, *Path of the Just*, 15.

Action or Patience?

Toward the end of the last chapter, we raised the issue of choosing between patience and action. Remember that if we cannot act, patience is our last resort. If we can and should act, however, enthusiasm is called for. I have created a decision tree to help you decide whether to act or be patient; see figure 8.

Let me give you an example. Let's say you are waiting in line for something. You have an opportunity to run to another line ahead of the people in front of you. On the tree there is the question, "Are my needs more important than the needs of the people in front of me?" If no, I should exercise patience and wait my turn. After all, they got there first, fair and square. On the other hand, if your wife is going into labor and you need something to bring to the delivery room, your priorities are higher and it is okay to ask to move ahead in line. Patience is not the right thing to do when action is needed.

Enthusiasm and Laziness

Sometimes we don't take action out of general sluggishness, which has nothing to do with patience but everything to do with enthusiasm out of balance.

In *Path of the Just*, Rabbi Luzzatto argues that humans do not like work and thus naturally are lazy. Moreover, we need constant vigilance and reinforcement to overcome our nature and the influence of the evil inclination as it tries to prevent us from doing good in the world. He writes, "If one becomes lax and indolent and does not act rigorously in pursuing [good deeds] and in holding on to them, he will find himself empty."[80] For example, the stereotypical couch potato is not waiting for anything; he's just passing time. The book of Proverbs warns against such a lifestyle: "A little sleep, a little slumber, a little folding of the hands to rest—and poverty will come on you like a thief and scarcity like an armed man."[81]

---

80 Luzzatto, *Path of the Just*, 37–38.
81 Proverbs 6:10–11, New International Version.

Figure 8: *Patience or Enthusiasm Decision Tree*

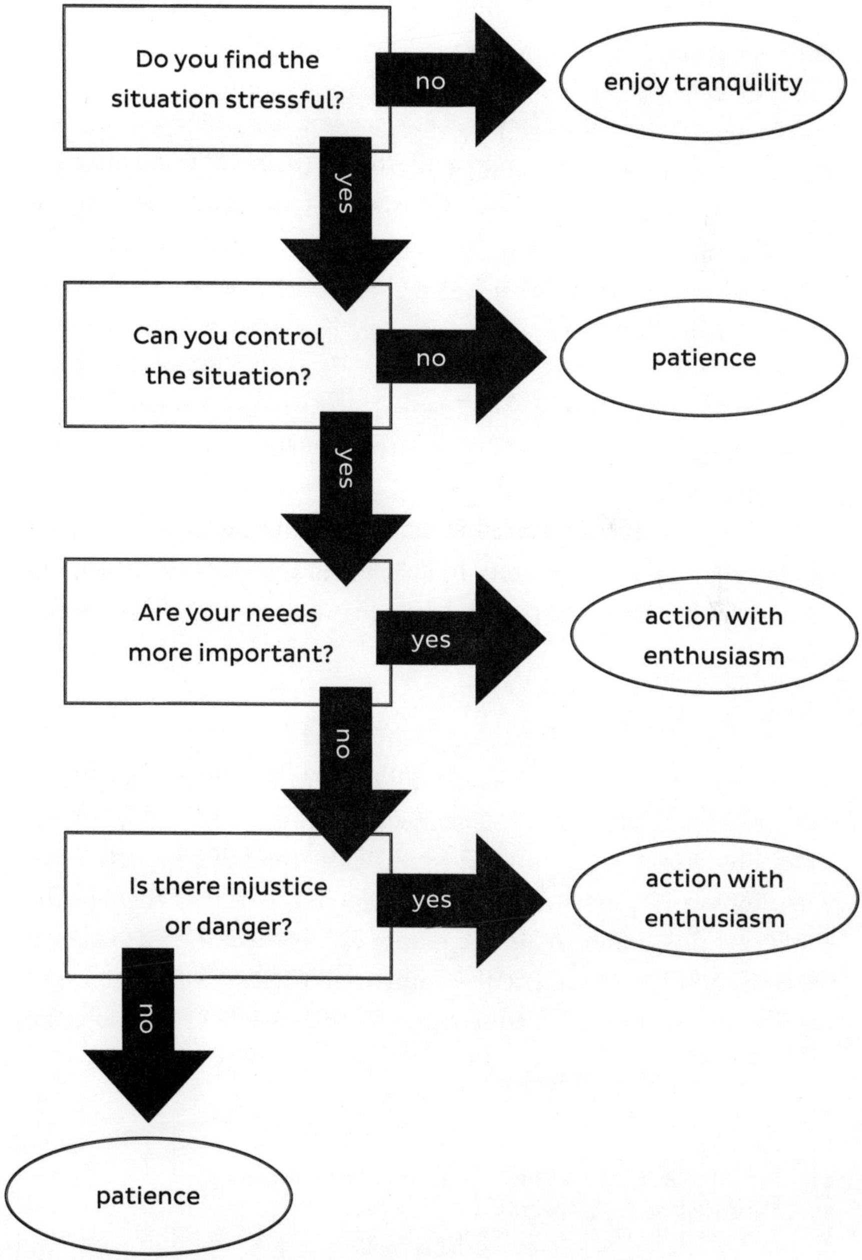

The evil inclination provides rationalizations and thoughts that drive down our energy. For example, when I don't want to get up and change the cat litter, I might say to myself, "I'll do it later, during the next commercial." Then, "I'll do it after the show." And then, "If it does not get done until morning, will it really hurt them?" The harm is that I lost an opportunity to do my best to care for my animals. What good comes from sitting and watching another fifteen minutes of the show that I already have recorded on the DVR? I should be taking that opportunity to do what I need to do. Furthermore, I also lose an opportunity to feel good while doing it!

Rabbi Luzzatto argued that we need the trait of enthusiasm to fight the evil inclination.[82] He points to a story in the Talmud about a man who did not want to leave his room and gave a litany of excuses to justify his position. First there is a lion in the street, then he says his door is locked. After each excuse is shot down, he finally says, "I would like to sleep a little more."[83]

Do these voices sound at all familiar? There is always some reason not to attack each opportunity to do good in the world. As it says in Proverbs, "The indolent person is wiser in his own eyes than seven sages."[84]

Run to Do Good

One of the ways that we practice Mussar is to follow the example of role models. Abraham is a role model for enthusiasm.[85] For example, right after Abraham circumcised himself at the age of ninety-nine, when three strangers arrived at his camp, in the heat of the day, the Torah says that Abraham hurried to take care of them. He hurried over to wash their feet; he hurried to Sarah to ask her to bake bread; and he ran to select a young and tender calf for dinner.[86] In addition, the

---

82 Luzzatto, *Path of the Just*, 37.

83 Ibid., 52.

84 Proverbs 26:16, as translated in Luzzatto, *Path of the Just*, 40.

85 *The Ways of the Tzaddikim*, 283.

86 Genesis 18:2–8, New International Version.

Torah says that Abraham "rose early in the morning" to fulfill a painful request from God.[87] King David, another biblical luminary, wrote, "I will hasten and not delay to obey Your commands."[88] I think the spirit of what David is saying is that we should immediately follow God's teachings without delay, or, as it says in *The Ways of the Tzaddikim*, "If [an opportunity to do good] comes to hand, do not let it go stale."[89] Whatever your thoughts on Divinity, we need look no further than the Golden Rule to see the merit in running to do good.

In a practical sense, "running to do good" can be one of the most joyous Mussar practices. For example, once during a Q&A session at a forum at my synagogue, an elderly man raised his hand to ask a question. I was holding the microphone from a previous question and the person next to me held out her hand to begin passing it up and over at least five rows to get to him. The phrase "run to do good" popped into my head. Since I was on the aisle and the man raising his hand was in the front row, I quickly jogged over to where he was sitting to deliver the microphone. He gave me a huge smile, as did the people sitting around me.

My experience was very much in line with the description of alacrity by Rabbi Luzzatto, who wrote, "If one is enthusiastic in his performance of a *mitzvah* [commandment], he will find that when he quickens his external [physical] movement he will thereby cause his inner fervor to be aroused."[90]

Enthusiasm for the Wrong Things

Sometimes we are very enthusiastic and pour energy into the wrong things. For example, what are the priorities of the person described below by someone I interviewed for my previous book?[91]

---

87   Genesis 22:3.
88   Psalms 119:60, New International Version.
89   Zaloshinsky, *The Ways of the Tzaddikim*, 291.
90   Luzzatto, *Path of the Just*, 44. Note that alacrity and enthusiasm are alternate English translations of the same Hebrew word for this soul trait.
91   Marcus, *Busting Your Corporate Idol*, 16.

He said, "I knew this payroll manager who had two young girls, but he thrilled to the fact that the CFO of the company could call him Thursday night at nine and he would be there to pick up the phone. That thrilled him, as he seemed to have the company running in his veins. He had little to no quality time with his kids. I do not get that at all. Personally, I quit that company for quality of life, and I took a pay cut to do it."

There was a time in my life when I was like that payroll manager. I put all of my energy into my employer. Whenever I had a choice to make, I chose to work over spending time with my family. I put so much energy into work that it came to dominate all of my thoughts. I would think about work every night at dinner, even when I was home with the family. One of the things that drove me was a desire to revolutionize medicine through personal genetics. Ultimately, though, my energy was going toward the wrong things. In fact, one of the sins we atone for on Yom Kippur is zeal for bad causes.

Daily Practice

Mantra

Enthusiasm is a soul trait that lends itself to several alternative mantras. Which of these fits you best?

"Make the most of every moment."

"Look before you leap."

"Run to do good."

I particularly like "run to do good" because it follows directly from a teaching by Ben Azzai in the Talmud: "Run to pursue a minor *mitzvah* [commandment], and flee from a transgression. For a mitzvah brings another mitzvah, and a transgression brings another transgression."[92]

Choose a mantra, write it on an index card, and put it somewhere you'll see it in the morning. As an extra burst of enthusiasm, make a second copy of your mantra and put it in your car.

---

92   *Pirkei Avot* 4:2.

Observe

Rabbi Dov Ber of Radoshitz would waken his roommates with the call, "Wake up, my brothers! A guest you've never seen has arrived. Once he leaves, you will never see him again. [Who is the guest?] Today."[93] As you go through your day, use Rabbi Radoshitz's words and the questions below as a yardstick to evaluate your enthusiasm balance.

- Do you treat each moment as a unique opportunity to do good?

- How does your enthusiasm wax and wane over the course of the day? When do you feel the heaviness of inaction gaining ascendance? When are you just phoning it in?

- Alternatively, what are the things that you are most passionate about? Are you putting your energy into the right things or are you squandering your enthusiasm on activities or causes that do not align with your core values?

Write down your observations in your journal.

From My Journal

The first time I wrote in my journal about enthusiasm, it was winter and the lack of light left me battling a feeling of heaviness. Having the mantra of "just do it" gave me a framework to fight the sluggishness. For example, it helped me to get my daily blog posts out. One day I wrote the following:

Enthusiasm is hard when I'm sick with a cold. It helped me unload the dishwasher, clean the cat litter, and start sorting my papers, but heaviness took over. I stopped and did not call my friend. I had various internal excuses. I must try more tomorrow.

---

93   *Pirkei Avos Treasury*, 43.

Chapter 7

The next day I continued:

Enthusiasm reminded me to clean the cat litter, talk to my wife about our daughter's dance class, and bring the pile of books downstairs for the library. Then I took a nap. Being sleepy is not the same as being lazy. Sometimes taking a nap is the right thing to do. I would say the greatest achievement from my practice of enthusiasm is that I started saying "I love you" to my dad. We are one of those families where the feeling is there but the words are not spoken. It felt really good for me to speak the words.

Act

Enthusiasm offers wonderful practices to change your life. Here are a few ideas:

- **Get more sleep.** According to the CDC, 30 percent of Americans are sleep deprived. If you are among this group (as I once was), you won't realize how poorly you are functioning until you become rested. An overworked life with not enough sleep is a sign of insufficient priorities and an attempt to put your energy into too many different things. Getting more sleep will make your life richer and more effective.

- **Conduct an enthusiasm inventory.** In your journal, write about the things that give you energy and the things in your life that suck up your energy.

- **Track roadblocks to positive energy.** Bring positive energy to everything you do. For many people, after a day or two, this will become very difficult. Something will happen and the habits of negative energy will re-assert themselves. When this happens, look inside and write down the feelings, then revisit them as your Mussar vocabulary grows in future chapters.

- **Just do it when it comes time to do a task and you feel that heaviness starting to set in.** Do not procrastinate; just get it done. There are so few moments in our life. Each moment that we waste because we are slugging along is a lost opportunity to do something good.

- **Be grateful.** One way to keep your energy up is to practice gratitude (chapter 12). One of the reasons that we lose energy is that we start to take what we have in this world for granted. By practicing gratitude we can begin to notice the ordinary. We can begin to appreciate that we have a warm bed and good food to eat. We can appreciate our friends and remember that we are lucky to be alive. Right now, I am grateful for my cat who keeps trying to distract me while I am writing the book. I am grateful for having a home and living in a place that has good weather. When we are grateful moment to moment, we are filled with enthusiasm to do what needs to be done.

- **Stick with positive people.** *The Ways of the Tzaddikim* teaches that we should not associate with people given to idle talk, and to actively separate oneself from the company of the wicked.[94] In the Middle Ages, like today, a person's conduct was highly influenced by his or her peers. Who are the people in your life who bring out the best in you? In particular, who has good energy? Are there people you associate with who carry around negative energy? In your journal, write about one person who brings positive energy and one who brings negative energy. Reach out to strengthen the relationships with the positive influences, and begin to distance yourself from people who are too negative.

---

94   Zaloshinsky, *The Ways of the Tzaddikim*, 289, 293.

Trust in God
but tie your camel.

Chapter Eight

◆

Trust

I am not naturally a trusting person. I have had certain experiences in my life that made me wary of other people. As a result, I have a tendency to jump to conclusions that are not always kind to others. The assumption below helps explain what is going on.

Assumption: We Are Driven By a Conflict Between Good Inclination and Evil Inclination

When I was a young man, my suspicious nature was particularly evident when I was dating. I never wanted to pay for dinner out of fear that my date was trying to take advantage of me. In hindsight, this severely cut down on the number of second dates. (I did, however, pay for dinner on the first date with my future wife.) This lack of trust led to all kinds of fears that came out in other ways.

Every time a woman was late for a date or didn't return my phone call right away, a little fear pinged inside of me. The fear led me to be impatient and to start thinking, "She must not be interested in me. She obviously has something better to do." When the date did arrive, I was nervous and anxious, which got the evening off on the wrong foot.

Fear comes from the evil inclination. Fear is a primitive emotion, critical for survival, but in this case it was running unchecked and leading me to take actions that held me back socially. If my good inclination had been stronger, I would have been able to counter fears, for example, by reminding myself that traffic is always heavy in a big city, which has nothing to do with me personally. As you study trust, look for the fingerprints of the evil inclination in your actions, and look to your good inclination for guidance and courage.

What Is Trust?

Mussar teaches that trust is short for trust in God, which brings with it a powerful sense of confidence. Or, if you are unsure of your feelings about Divinity, it is trusting in a higher purpose that things will work themselves out. Rabbi Bachya ibn Paquda wrote that trust is "tranquility of the soul [based on]…reliance on the one in whom he trusts to do what is good and right for him."[95] In more modern terms, ibn Paquda is saying that if you believe God has your back, worry will disappear.

If you are unsure about Divinity, remember that Mark Twain once said, "I have been through some terrible things in my life, some of which actually happened." Most of the time when our fears put us through mental gymnastics about all of the horrible things that could go wrong, very few of those things actually happen. Trust allows us to believe in a benevolent universe where things are going to work out most of the time so we can let go of the string of fears. Or, put another way, trust is a belief that when bad things happen, it is a blessing in disguise. Thus, when I wasn't getting second dates, it was a good thing because it kept me available so that I could start dating the woman I eventually married.

Trusting God as a life strategy is very alien to many people in America. In fact, two Reform rabbis I know who teach Mussar told me that they find trust very hard to practice. Trust is so difficult that it is often

---

95   ibn Paquda, *Duties of the Heart*, 365.

one of the last soul traits covered in most modern Mussar books. I put it as the fourth soul trait for the following reasons:

- **Trust is a cure for fear.** Fear is the favorite weapon of the evil inclination, and without trust our spiritual journey will be inhibited.

- **Trust can help bring many other soul traits into balance.** We'll call on it throughout the rest of the book.

- **Trust is hard and counterintuitive, so it is better to start working on it early.** We all need practice.

Many Mussar masters argue that faith in God is required for Mussar practice in general and is a precursor to trust.[96] I disagree, which is why faith is not one of the soul traits I teach. If this describes you, I have good news: you are in a position to begin to see benefits quickly from bringing your trust toward balance.

Spectrum of Trust

fear ← too little | *Trust* | too much → recklessness

When we have too much trust, we become reckless. We can sit back and just let God take care of everything, giving us the freedom to drive too fast and drink too much. The financial collapse in 2008 showed the danger of too much trust. We are constantly reminded that we live in an interconnected world. We have credit cards, online access to our money, and can pay for coffee by scanning our phone. Banks trade money all over the world in seconds. When we put the little plastic card in the slot, we trust that we'll be able to fill up our gas tank. Everything works just fine—until it didn't in 2008.

---

96   Morinis, *Everyday Holiness*, 210.

The financial system became so complex that even the experts did not understand what was happening or how it worked. They had blind trust that the system would work out and the market would take care of everything. By blindly trusting the system, they were not doing their due diligence, and they missed the fact that some of our biggest financial institutions were running up huge debts. When the markets started to turn, our financial system came close to collapse, millions of people lost their jobs, and the United States endured the biggest financial hardship since the Great Depression.

If we had trusted less in our financial systems and the people running them, we would have demanded checks and balances to prevent the reckless lending that got us into trouble.

On the other hand, too little trust means that we are ruled by fear, concerned that something could go wrong at every turn. We fear that if we don't get everything exactly right, then disaster is going to strike. By trusting in God or something higher than ourselves, we do not need to fear because we know that eventually things are going to work out.

The practice of trust has helped me quiet my mind when it starts to race about all the things I have to do or all the things that could go wrong.

The Blessing in Disguise

Have you ever been laid off? At the time it can feel like a horrible disaster, yet years later, many of these same people will say that the layoff was the best thing that ever happened to them. For example, the layoff got them out of a toxic situation and they found a new job they absolutely loved. For others, a layoff was an opportunity to start their own business or go back to school and change careers. Or maybe they met their future spouse in line at the unemployment office. We do not know how things will turn out. In the middle of a project, things usually look like an absolute mess. When the project is over we have something really great. With trust, we can have the patience to see how our life can play out.

Trusting God When Bad Things Happen

Now, a natural question to ask, and many people have, is whether we are supposed to trust God when something really awful happens.

Personal tragedy can make the idea of "trust in God" even harder to take. In his book *Everyday Holiness*, Alan Morinis shares an example of someone who asked if she was supposed to trust a God who allowed her ex-husband to sexually assault her daughter.[97]

It is very hard to think of a God who allows someone's daughter to be raped and think that somehow some good in the universe will result. But don't we see good things coming out of tragedy all the time? Sometimes parents who have lost a child, or someone who has been a victim of the unthinkable, create a foundation to help victims or help prevent a similar tragedy from happening in the future.

I personally don't believe that the Holocaust or assaults are part of God's plan. I think God's plan is to allow a universe to function according to the laws of nature and free will. People are free to choose evil. God cannot prevent the evil without taking away our ability to choose, but this doesn't mean that God is absent. I trust that God is always there to hold my hand, to give me the strength to get through whatever life may bring.

I see God's hand in the good things that can come out of tragedy. If you are unsure of Divinity, look to the words of Mr. Rogers, who taught us to look for the helpers after a disaster because his mother told him there are always people there to help.[98]

Would You Want to Live in a World Where God Prevents Calamities?

I suspect that the spiritual shadow of the Holocaust was a source of great angst for many throughout the latter part of the twentieth century and is a reason why so many Jews lost faith or lost touch with the spiritual side of our tradition.

---

97 Morinis, *Everyday Holiness*, 210.
98 Rogers, "Tragic Events."

Chapter 8

It is not uncommon for people to say something like:

- "I cannot believe in a God who would allow the Holocaust to happen."

- "How could God have allowed Rwanda/Serbia/ISIS/Cambodia/Stalin and a host of other genocides to take place?"

- "My sister died of cancer, and since then I am done with God."

I asked my class if they wanted to live in a world where God prevented the Holocaust. One person piped up immediately, *"Yes,* I want God to have prevented the Holocaust."

"How would that work?" I asked.

"God would have prevented it," she answered.

"How? What would God have done?" I persisted.

Another student of mine sat there with a growing sense of discomfort on her face. She finally blurted out, "I would not want to live in that kind of world because God could not prevent those events without taking away my free will."

Think about it for a moment. What could God have done? Struck down Hitler with lightning? To do so would violate the laws of nature. Maybe God would have made Hitler not hate the Jews? That would indeed have limited Hitler's free will.

The Talmud teaches that the angels are jealous of humans because humans have free will and the angels have to do whatever God tells them to.[99] God created a universe where people have the right to choose to commit genocide and where people have the right to choose to stand by and do nothing. It is a convenient excuse—and, frankly, a cop-out—to blame God for the ills of the world.

Another student didn't want to live in a world where God prevents evil because we would also lose good in the process.

---

99   Shabbat 88b. Shurpin, "Can Angels Sin?"

The first student's eyes lit up when he said this. She shared a story of a time when one of her kids was in the hospital on the first night of Hanukkah. The whole family was in the room, and they were feeling very down. Out of the blue, the Rabbinic chaplain walked in carrying a menorah. Together, the family lit the Hanukkah candles. She said it was a beautiful moment of togetherness she'll never forget. Yes, being in the hospital on a holiday was scary, painful, and a bummer, yet it allowed an unforgettable moment of goodness to come into the world, an unlooked-for godsend.

Examples from the Workplace

In her book *The Improvisation Edge*, Karen Hough tells the story of someone who had a trust issue in the workplace. This person had not seen her husband in a week and worked from nine in the morning until midnight every day, saying, "There is no one else who can do this. I cannot trust anyone to get it done right, and if this work does not happen, it could be disastrous to [the company]."[100]

What soul traits are in play here?

- Clearly this person does not have enough trust. While she describes this as not trusting others to do the job right, she also does not trust the universe to bring about a good outcome. The word "disastrous" indicates that she is reacting out of fear, and the cure for fear is trust.

- She has too little humility. She thought she was absolutely essential. I'm sorry, but no one person is essential for a company.

- Too little patience. She was not patient enough to wait for others to learn enough to help her.

- There is also an issue about misplaced enthusiasm. She was putting all of her energy into the company and not sufficient energy into the relationship with her husband.

---

100   Hough, *The Improvisation Edge*, 11.

Notice that the practice of trust would help her bring each of these other soul traits toward balance. She would have had a tool to unwind her faulty assumptions. For example, she would know that God is in charge of the universe, and thus the fate of the company was in God's hands and not hers. If you are unsure of Divinity, you can remember that each of us play a very small part in the world, and often our contribution is far smaller than we think it is. Moreover, if the fate of a company really depended on a single person, it would mean that the business was weak to begin with.

Too much trust can also be a problem in the workplace. Vijay, a laboratory technician in a biotech company, was extremely enthusiastic about his employer and always worked hard to do his best. One day a scientist came along and asked him to make a change in the way inventory was calculated. This change led to an inventory shortfall, as it covered the scientist's secret program to send inventory to a customer for free. Because Vijay trusted the wrong person, Vijay lost his job. If Vijay had a little more experience and less blind trust, he would have been able to avoid that situation.[101]

Whether at work or at home, when it comes to trust, our challenge is to figure out if we have too much or too little trust, and to take a small action to move toward balance.

Daily Practice

Mantra

I think the mantra that best represents trust is one I learned from the Islamic world. I have translated this into English as "trust in God but tie your camel."[102]

Trust in something higher is key for getting through life without fear and worry. At the same time, we cannot expect God to do all the work. We still have to do our part. In the example above, Vijay did not

---

101 Marcus, *Busting Your Corporate Idol*, 58–60.
102 The original saying is "trust in Allah but tie your camel."

tie his camel; a few discerning questions would have prevented his subsequent hardship.

In your life you might not tie your camel because you trust that things will be okay, only to wake up in the morning and find that your camel is gone. This isn't because the universe hates you; it is because you did not do your part. On the flip side, you might spend so much energy lashing your camel in place that you end up rushing to get your tent pitched before dark.

Observe

Look for opportunities during the day to observe how your trust soul trait is in play. For example, did you feel suspicious when someone asked you to lunch? Perhaps you've found yourself micromanaging an employee or blindly saying yes to whatever you are asked to do.

In addition, look for times when you are worried about what will happen in the future. Is that something you can control? Nine times out of ten, the answer is going to be no. Write about your experience in your journal.

From My Journal

I tried the practice of asking God for help today. It worked some. I prayed and then found some missing documents and my copy of The Black Swan; *I prayed and found a good parking spot. I said thank you each time. It was rough for me to get my blog post written. I asked God to help me get through the next five minutes and it helped me make progress.*

Act

Trust, because it is difficult and outside of our comfort zone, may require a greater effort than normal. If this is true for you, the good news is that there is a lot of room for growth and a great opportunity for a shorter-term impact on your life. Here are a few ideas for ways to practice trust:

- **Ask God for help when faced with a challenge.** The outcome may be what you wanted or it may not be. Whatever happens, say thank you. You may be skeptical about divine intervention; I am as well. At the same time, I've seen this work again and again. By asking for help, we are opening ourselves to a positive energy. Maybe we are asking the divine spark within to help give us the energy to tackle something we do not want to do. Maybe asking will give you the patience to get through an unpleasant situation. Don't worry about how it works; just give it a try. You'll be amazed at the results.

- **Use a mantra to counter worry.** When you start to worry, repeat the mantra "trust in God but tie your camel." Put a rubber band around your wrist to remind you to practice trust. I wear a bracelet with a hand charm (a hamsa) to remind me that God is always there to hold my hand. In times of stress I hold on to the tiny hand.

- **Surrender your need for a particular outcome.** Rabbi Yosef Hurwitz (1849–1919) taught, "A person who tries to practice trust in God while leaving himself a backup plan is like a person who tries to learn how to swim but insists on keeping one foot on the ground."[103] If you are like me, you fall more on the "tie your camel" side of the trust spectrum. We tie and tie and tie in a vain effort to make things turn out the way we want them to. We only need to take the next step for us, which means tie less. How? Surrender expectations about the outcome. Maybe it will work as you want it to; maybe not. Chances are, even if it doesn't come out as you expect, things will be okay. Try surrendering the outcome and see what happens.

- **Focus on the needs of other people if you have too much trust.** Contemporary Mussar leader Rabbi Ira Stone teaches that our primary task in Mussar practice is to bear the burden

---

103 Morinis, *Every Day, Holy Day*, 150.

of the other.[104] This is not a task that we can outsource to the Divine (or the universe, if we are unsure of the Divinity). If you tend toward too much trust, I suggest that you take inspiration from the teaching of Rabbi Stone to proactively look for opportunities to help other people.[105]

104 Stone, *A Responsible Life*, 318.
105 Luzzatto, *Mesillat Yesharim: The Path of the Upright*.

Sustain others without the thought of reward,
even if they don't deserve it.

Chapter Nine

◆

Loving-Kindness

I went into the weeks of loving-kindness with some trepidation. I have a temper and am uncomfortable with things that I consider soft and mushy. Therefore, I thought I was in for another shellacking. Much to my surprise, loving-kindness turned out to be one of my strengths.

Assumption: We All Have Free Will But It Is Not Always Accessible

What does it mean to have free will? It means that in any given situation we can choose what to do and how to do it. However, not all choices are the same. For example, if we take the path of least resistance, are we really choosing? Certainly it is not the same to let gravity carry you down as it is to decide to turn and strike off on your own.

Some of the things we do out of obligation are along the path of least resistance. Paying our taxes and stopping at a red light both fall under this category. If for some reason we decide not to pay taxes or not to stop at the red light, it feels like more of a deliberate choice because we are not following the path of least resistance.

As we will see in the next section, an act of loving-kindness requires that we step off the path of least resistance. To practice loving-kindness is to look for choice points that go out of our way to sustain others.

What Is Loving-Kindness?

Loving-kindness is the trait of doing selfless acts to help sustain other people where you do not expect anything in return. Judaism teaches that the world stands on three things: Torah, service of God, and acts of loving-kindness.[106] Thus, when we choose to perform an act of loving-kindness, we are choosing to help sustain and build the world. What a great image: building the world through acts of kindness. What image does that evoke for you? I have a physical image of each act of kindness as a physical brick that builds a strong foundation on which we walk. I see the bricks falling quickly into place and a great paradise arising that morphs into trees and beauty and art. I also see a metaphorical world where doing acts of loving-kindness creates the kind of world we want to live in, where people go out of their way to sustain others.

Acts of loving-kindness are not random acts of kindness. As Rabbi Janet Marder taught me, they are instead *deliberate* acts of kindness. Do you see the difference? We are not doling out kind acts willy-nilly. Rather, we are looking for opportunities to perform a kindness that will affect other people in a meaningful way.

Have you ever seen the movie *Pay It Forward,* starring Kevin Spacey? It is about a kid who does a school project about paying it forward when someone does something nice for you. You do not reciprocate but you do something nice for someone else. In the movie there is a chain reaction of "paying it forward" that crosses the country, which includes someone giving away a sports car. There have been recent real-world examples as well. For example, in 2014 378 people paid for the coffee for the person behind them in a drive-through Starbucks.[107] Paying it forward gives a feeling of well-being to all involved.

---

106 *Pirkei Avot* 1:2.
107 Firozi, "378 People 'Pay It Forward' at Starbucks."

Spectrum of Loving-Kindness

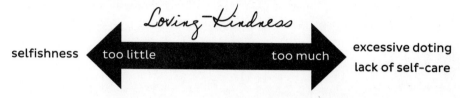

As with all soul traits, too much loving-kindness is a negative, as it leads to excessive doting on other people and a lack of self-care. A friend of mine who works in hospice told me that the most important interview question he asks is about self-care. If the candidates don't have a practice of self-care, he won't hire them because he knows they will burn out.

What happens if we have too little loving-kindness? We are selfish and mean. Because we are not kind to others, people will not be kind to us and we end up angry and alienated, much like Scrooge in the Dickens book *A Christmas Carol*. Everything becomes a quid pro quo, and there is too much focus on how we can get ahead.

Traditional Acts of Loving-Kindness

What does it mean that the world is built on loving-kindness? As I wrote earlier in the chapter, it implies a sustaining activity of some kind that goes beyond what we would normally do. The best way to understand the concept is to look at examples.

Rabbi Abraham Yachnes explains that helping someone carry a heavy load in the direction you were already going is not an act of loving-kindness. After all, you are expected to help someone if it doesn't take you out of your way. To qualify as an act of loving-kindness, you need to help someone carry the load in the opposite direction of where you were planning to go.[108] In a similar way, while it is nice to give a neighbor a ride home, it only qualifies as loving-kindness if you are driving someone home who lives on the opposite side of town.

---

108 Morinis, *Everyday Holiness*, 188.

Chapter 9

The Torah uses the Hebrew word for loving-kindness 245 times, often as an attribute of God.[109] Stop for a moment and think about that. Because the lesson is repeated 245 times, it must be absolutely fundamental that God is loving and kind. The Talmud lists the following as examples of ways we can emulate God's loving-kindness:[110]

- Visiting the sick

- Clothing the naked

- Comforting the bereaved

- Caring for the dead

If you are unsure of Divinity, let the universal power of love guide you to kindly nurture those in need. Allow love to take you off the path of least resistance so you may find those who need your support.

You may find one or more things on this list unpleasant or stressful. After all, hospitals are not pleasant places to be, and it can be hard to be in a room full of grieving people. Yet each of these acts makes a profound affect on the recipient and truly does make the world a better place. For example, I recently visited a friend who was recovering from a heart attack he suffered at a young age. He said to me, "Greg, I never got this 'visiting the sick' thing until I was sick myself. It means so much to me that people would take time out of their busy lives to come and see me."

Some people make it a regular practice to visit sick people in our synagogue. That is too big a step for me to take right now. For me, the right step is to visit anyone I even remotely know when they are in the hospital. When a close relative had a heart attack while visiting, he seemed amazed that I came to see him every day in the hospital. It was inconvenient, but I didn't hesitate because it is part of my Mussar practice. As I look back on it, there was a certain freedom in deciding ahead of time that I would visit every day. I could plan ahead, and I

---

109 Ibid., 185.
110 Sotah 14a.

never had any angst day-to-day about whether I should go. I knew that he appreciated it, and it felt right for me to be there, too.

Caring for the dead is something that we outsource in America to professionals. I was amazed to learn that in at least some Israeli Ortho-dox communities, the practice of caring for the dead rests within the community. This includes not only digging the grave but also prepar-ing the body. A student of mine traveled to Israel for his sister-in-law's funeral. She lived in a Modern Orthodox community, and he volun-teered to help dig her grave. He shared that it was one of the most meaningful things he had ever done.

Comforting the bereaved is something we can all do. Writer Anita Diamant shared her struggle to comfort a friend who had lost a baby.[111] Diamant described being "in mourning" as a parallel universe where being in the shadow of death is not a metaphor. Her friend told her that every gesture of support, even if it was a phone call or email to say "I'm sorry," counted for a lot because it gave her a connection to the living world. Diamant described her struggle to not try cheering her friend up as she held her friend's hand while she cried. While I have not been in those exact shoes, I know what it feels like to want to cheer someone else up. In part, it is because we want to feel better. It is really heavy to be there with someone who is in such terrible pain. Diamant's act of selfless loving-kindness leaves me in a kind of help-less awe.

The one step I have been able to take is to attend the traditional mourning gathering, or shivah, at the home of the bereaved whenever I have the slightest connection to the person who passed. Sometimes people seem surprised to see me, but pleasantly so. I'll be honest: it is no fun to go. It is really heavy, and I drive over with a sense of dread. Yet, at the same time, it isn't about me. I am there as a member of the community, and people really appreciate it.

---

111 Diamant, *Pitching My Tent*, 104–106.

Loving the Right Things for the Right Reasons

Loving-kindness drives us to do things for others in a selfless way. Yet not all selfless activity is loving-kindness, and not all selflessness is healthy. Below is a story that I shared in my previous book that is relevant to loving-kindness.[112]

A retired female biotech executive described her feelings about work as follows:

"There were stages in my job where I loved my work. I would get in early, stay late, and I thoroughly enjoyed it. I thought I was making a contribution, and it all felt right to me. What made it good was the corporate leadership. When I was really clear in my scientific heart, we had strengths to address [the goals of the company]."

Later, she told me more about her home life.

"I would go home, have dinner, and then the CEO would call me to rehash strategy. The CEO later asked me if my divorce was from job stress. It was not. I was working hard, but that was not what caused the marriage to crumble."

We discussed her home life for a while, and I agreed with her assessment: it was not that work had caused the marriage to crumble. In fact, I believe that work had become a refuge from a marriage that was crumbling.

The story itself reminds me that love is a verb, not a feeling. Love is how we act toward another. When given the choice between spending time with her family or spending time working, she worked. In a sense, she was building the foundation of her professional world instead of building the foundation of her personal world. Again, in her case, we should not judge because it is not for us to decide for others how they should make their choices.

I've been in strategy discussions like the ones she refers to, and I know they are fun and energizing. Fortunately, my marriage has been good, and work did not become a refuge from an unhappy home life, or at least not on a regular basis. There were times when things got crazy

---

112 Marcus, *Busting Your Corporate Idol*, 45.

and hectic with two working parents raising two small kids, and I was happy to get out of the house. When those spiritual tests come up for me today—when the stress and craziness of life make me want to bolt for the door—I try to stay in the situation as an act of loving-kindness.

Loving-Kindness for Effect, Not a Scorecard

There is a natural joy that comes from doing things for other people. Judaism teaches that joy is something that exists within us. When we get out of our own way, joy can emerge. Now, a cynic might say that acts of loving-kindness are actually acts of selfishness since we derive pleasure from doing them. Mussar addresses this concern by instructing us that we are not allowed to do acts of kindness simply for the pleasure it gives us; it has to be about the other person. I think it is even simpler: if we are chasing that good feeling by trying to do things for others, we won't get the same kind of feeling that we get when we are selfless. We can't chase or evoke the satisfaction from helping others. It only arises when we are genuinely giving kindness from the heart in order to serve others in a selfless way.

We perform acts of loving-kindness for the feeling created in other people. Think about that feeling when someone just out of the blue has done something super nice for you. It feels not only great, but uplifting. Once when I was walking home after dropping my daughter off at school, one of the other parents out of the blue turned around and said to me, "I so admire you for writing a book." At the time, I was having writer's block and was starting to wonder if I would ever finish my first book. Her unexpected, kind words totally revitalized me and gave me a boost that helped me bust through the writer's block.

Ideally, we will not be doing acts of loving-kindness simply to fill our Mussar scorecard. At the same time, if loving-kindness is new to you, performing loving-kindness to fill your scorecard is exactly what you should be doing. We all start at different places; if practicing loving-kindness will feel awkward and forced for you, that's okay because that is where you are today. Take the small, forced action. Each act of mindful loving-kindness will leave a small trace on your soul, and over time acts of loving-kindness will come like second nature.

Finding the Right Step for You

How can you bring more loving-kindness into your life? Starting from where you are, what is the right next act? Sometimes when people hear about doing acts of kindness, they look for what I call the grand gesture. For example, ever hear a story about a person who anonymously pays for the dinner of someone else in a restaurant? Some people hear this story and applaud. For me, it brings up skepticism, and I feel disempowered. I begin to wonder if the grand gesture is about ego, where the benefactor is showing off for his date. These particular judgmental thoughts have everything to do with my personal spiritual curriculum. More generally, however, I think paying for dinner anonymously is both expensive and a very big step, too big for me today, and perhaps too big for you as well.

Part of the reason why I dislike grand gestures like anonymously paying for a stranger's dinner is that I find them overwhelming. I can never see myself randomly paying for someone else's dinner. For me, if the bar for an act of loving-kindness is to buy someone a free dinner anonymously, I would just get discouraged and not do any acts of loving-kindness at all! Mussar is not about the grand gesture. It is about doing that next step that is right for you.

For me, the right next step is to bring the bowl of kitchen scraps out to the compost bin every night. My wife doesn't like the smell and reminds me that it is especially bad before she has had her coffee. Part of me was thinking, "Why don't you stop complaining and just bring them out?" I decided, however, that I would bring them out as an act of loving-kindness. I didn't say anything or make a big deal out of the practice. I just regularly empty the compost bowl before it gets stinky because I know it will make her unhappy to have bad smells in the kitchen. And I must say that it feels both good and empowering to do this for her.

Daily Practice

Mantra

Write the following mantra on an index card: "Sustain others without the thought of reward, even if they don't deserve it." Place it by your bedside or in the bathroom where you'll see it regularly. Chant the mantra to yourself for a few minutes to frame your day.

Observe

Observe how loving-kindness affects your thoughts, feelings, and actions over the course of the day. Be on the lookout for rationalizations that hold you back and prevent you from going the extra mile to support others. Rationalizations can include:

- It's not all that bad.

- Other people are there.

- I have too much going on to help this time.

- I wrote a check at the end of the year for a similar charity.

- How much difference can I make anyway?

Write about your observations and actions in your Mussar journal at night.

From My Journal

Today I started loving-kindness, and right away I got an email from the rabbi that they need people to cook and eat dinner with the homeless. Totally out of my comfort zone. I signed up because I am practicing loving-kindness, and clothing the poor is on the list. I am dreading it.

Something cool happened too. I've been holding off on certain book activities, waiting for the contract to be signed. Part of me knew that trust should lead me to just move ahead, especially because we agreed to all terms, but I didn't want to jinx things. Today I finally gave in and started to move forward. One hour after I started, I got an email that the contract was signed. Not a coincidence!

Act

What act of loving-kindness can you do to help sustain others? Not a big, grand gesture—something small to sustain someone close to you and not randomly but deliberately. Here are a few ideas:

- **Say yes to help.** Loving-kindness is a two-way interaction. Someone needs to give and someone needs to receive. How often does someone offer to help, and we reflexively say, "No, I've got it covered"? This is an unfortunate byproduct of the community-challenged state of America in the twenty-first century; we just are not used to asking for or receiving help. Every time we say no to help, we are denying someone else the opportunity to practice loving-kindness—and we deny an opportunity to be kind to ourselves.

- **Do more than your share at home.** Earlier in the chapter I shared how I empty the compost bowl because my wife doesn't like the smell. Try to identify a small thing that makes someone close to you unhappy, then find a way to remove the concern. What can you do to make the house cleaner or more peaceful? What is something that someone you care about really hates to do? Do it for them out of loving-kindness.

- **Love work less.** I used to consistently go above and beyond what was required of me at work. It took a toll on my health and home life. Love is a verb, and by "love work less" I mean do less work out of devotion in order to open up more time in your life for sleep, hobbies, and time with friends and family. Set a concrete step such as no phone calls or text messages during dinner.

- **Forgive someone out of loving-kindness even if you think they are at fault and should make the first move.** Kindness can lead you to begin to repair the relationship.

- **Visit or call someone who is sick.** Friend, coworker, acquaintance, or relative—usually someone will be under the weather in a given week. We live in overscheduled times. If you schedule a visit or even a few minutes for a phone call, that speaks volumes to the other person.

Distance yourself from falsehood.

Chapter Ten

◆

Truth

I loved telling the truth. I prided myself in saying the things others were afraid to say and thought this was one of my best traits. I was a walking lesson in honesty. What a shock I got when I started to study truth as part of my Mussar practice. I was giving so much truth that I lost sight of kindness.

Assumption: We All Share the Same Soul Traits and Have a Unique Measure of Each

People have different personalities, which lead to different reactions to similar situations. Our society focuses on differences in our psychological makeup to explain the different behaviors, yet on a spiritual level our makeup is the same. We all share the same soul traits, and the differences we see are like different settings on a dial. The measure of each trait determines what we do.

There might be someone who is a perpetual liar and you may think that they do not have a grain of truth in their body. That is not true. They do have truth; it is just dramatically out of balance. They, like all of us, have the ability to adjust the dial. Others have their truth setting set too high and come across in a painful and harshly blunt way. This type of person could do well by being less truthful. The important thing to remember is that all people share the trait and have the opportunity to practice Mussar and make adjustments.

What Is the Truth?

We think of the truth as a correct representation of an object, event, or feeling. Judaism, however, teaches that the truth is much more complicated because, as humans, we can only perceive a fraction of what is happening in the world. For example, you can have four people in a room participating in the same activity and each one could walk out of that room with an entirely different picture of what happened. Even in the best of circumstances, each person will tell a different story, and thus each person has their version of the truth in their own mind. Who is to say which one is right? They all are, in a sense, because each person experienced those events from a unique point of view and comes from a unique history.

In addition, human memory is faulty and is influenced by our experience and preconceived notions of the world. For example, if you show someone a photograph of an office and ask him five minutes later to list things he saw in the picture, a significant proportion will remember seeing a desk, even when no desk was in the picture. We have a vision of an office in our head from prior experience, and objects from the "office schema" will make their way into memory.[113]

So, given the human limitations on both perception and recall, where is this universal truth? Judaism teaches that only God sits upon the throne of truth. If I say that I saw a desk, was I being untruthful? No, I was telling my truth—which happened to be factually inaccurate.

---

113 Hockenbury, *Psychology*, 265.

Truth for God and Truth for the Rest of Us

As an abstract idea, we might believe that there is only one single truth. However, the very idea of a single truth is an illusion. To diverge for just a moment into the world of quantum physics, the Heisenberg Uncertainty Principle states that it is impossible to know a particle's precise position and momentum. In layman's terms, we can't know exactly where something is and precisely how fast it is going at the same time. While the math is complicated and way over my head, the takeaway for me is this: if a physicist cannot tell you the exact truth about an object, how can any of the rest of us expect to find exact truth in everyday life? Everything is an approximation.

Mussar (and Judaism) teaches that only God sits upon the throne of truth. In that sense, you could say that God does know what is true since God knows all things and can see from all perspectives simultaneously. The Hebrew word for truth is *emet*. In Hebrew emet is spelled by three letters: the first, middle, and last letters of the alphabet, in that order. The rabbis understand this to mean that God knows everything: the beginning, middle, and end.[114, 115]

If you are unsure about Divinity, the idea that the absolute truth is unknowable to humans still holds. We do not have the ability to simultaneously know the truth from all perspectives, and thus we have to make do with what we have. Even so, Mussar asks that we learn to appreciate the truth of other people.

Your task, then, as you practice truth over the next two weeks, is to try to see the truth through the eyes of the people around you.

114 Morinis, *Every Day, Holy Day*, 167.

115 A similar concept exists in Christianity: Jesus says, "I am the Alpha and the Omega, the First and the Last, the Beginning and the End" (Revelation 22:13, NIV). Alpha and omega are the first and last letters of the Greek alphabet.

Chapter 10

The Spectrum of Truth

erodes trust, a pillar of the world ← too little | too much → hurtful speech

Truth

If we have too much truth, the result may be unkind, hurtful speech. I see this in my kids all the time. I have two teenage daughters who sometimes snipe at each other. They will say something unkind about what the other one is wearing.

I yell out, "Don't say that about your sister."

Answer: "But it is true; that is what I am thinking."

In a calmer voice I explain, "Yes, you are speaking what you are truly thinking. It does not mean, however, that you should say it if it is unkind."

Would we really want to live in a world were we had to tell the absolute truth all the time? *The Invention of Lying* is a comedy that depicts a world where everyone tells the literal truth all the time. Imagine going on a date and hearing, "You're chubby and you have a snub nose." Or your date tells you, "We both know that one day you're going to lose your looks." This funny movie brings home the point that telling the absolute truth would not make a very good world. For example, there are times when we should withhold the truth in the name of kindness. Moreover, the Talmud teaches that it is okay to be untruthful in the name of peace in the house.

Too little truth means that we are dishonest. As Rabbi M. M. Levin points out, "If the liar speaks truthfully, no one believes him any longer."[116] This reflects a general lack of respect for people who tell lies. Rabbi Levin continues, explaining that liars are "despised even by those who benefit from their lies, and they pay them like one throws a carcass to a dog."[117] This trope continues to hold true today. For

---

116 Levin, *Cheshbon HaNefesh*, 175.
117 Ibid.

example, in the science fiction classic *Dune,* the Suk Doctor Yuh who betrayed the Atreides family is scornfully referred to by the people he helped as "the traitor."

My grandmother used to tell a story about a man who used to drive the babysitter home after she watched his kids. They started having an affair, and eventually he left his wife and married the babysitter. When they had children, it was always the wife who drove the sitter home. A man who would leave one wife for a babysitter would do it again. Notice how their world was undermined because there was too little truth—one marriage was destroyed, and the foundation of the new marriage was shaky.

Rabbi Simeon ben Gamliel said, "The world stands on three things: truth, justice, and peace. Truth brings justice, which results in peace."[118] And Rabbi Muna explains, "These three things are actually one. When justice is done, truth is served and peace is achieved."[119]

In addition to damaging our personal relationships, untruth also damages our spiritual relationships. The Talmud teaches that a liar cannot experience the Divine Presence.[120] Judaism teaches that experiencing the Divine Presence is feeling a real connection with the divine spark within. It can be experienced as a comfort, as a dissipation of loneliness, and/or as a feeling that all is well and will be okay.

If you are skeptical about Divinity and the Divine Presence, simply think of it as a calm feeling of inner peace. Lying is hard work. It often requires ever-greater webs of lies to prevent becoming discovered. Who can feel inner peace when in constant fear of discovery? As it says in Proverbs, "One who deceives his fellow through flattery is spreading a net for his own footsteps."[121]

---

118 Bialik and Ravnitsky, *Book of Legends,* 733:128.
119 Perek HaShalom 1:2 from http://tmt.urj.net/images/MT178-179.pdf.
120 Sotah 42a, http://www.come-and-hear.com/sotah/sotah_42.html.
121 Proverbs 29:5.

Chapter 10

Peace Before Truth

So far, our investigation of truth has been complicated. We've seen that the truth is hard to discern because we all have limited perceptions, and each of us will have an imperfect and biased view of the truth. In addition, we see that too little truth is undermining to the world, and too much truth can lead to harsh and alienating judgments. With only these teachings to go on, one might be tempted to freeze and never say or do anything from "analysis paralysis." Luckily, Judaism provides guidance on how we can evaluate whether to be truthful.

Our first lesson comes from Rabbi Hillel, who taught that one should always compliment a bride as beautiful on her wedding day.[122] If we bring this teaching into the modern world, the key lesson to remember is that we should consider the effect of our truth on another person. Weddings are a time of joy, and voicing a critical opinion about how the bride or groom looks, their taste, or their relatives could hurt someone's feelings, and thus it has no place on such a special day. Moreover, we should look for opportunities to proactively contribute to the joyous occasion by giving heartfelt compliments.

Second, the Talmud teaches that it is okay to deviate from the truth on account of peace.[123] This teaching in part derives from an incident in the Torah. Sarah essentially snickers when God says that Abraham will father a child at the age of ninety-nine. When Abraham asks what she is laughing at, God covers for her by saying that she was only laughing because she is old, and God does not repeat Sarah's thought that Abraham is old as well.[124] In this case, God told a white lie in order to spare Abraham's feelings—and to prevent a potential fight between Abraham and Sarah that might have precluded the conception of a child! Given that we are all descended from Isaac, I'm glad God stepped in.

Rabbi Jill Maderer explores a circumstance when a lie to an employer had a positive outcome.[125] A single mother of two and recent

---

122 Babylonian Talmud: Tractate Kethuboth Folio 17a.
123 Yebamoth 65b.
124 Genesis 18:12–13.
125 Maderer, "Turning Fate Into Destiny with a 'Sabbath Lie.'"

law-school graduate, she told her boss at a high-powered law firm that she did not work on Shabbat when, in fact, she had never observed Shabbat in her life. She told this lie in order to ensure that she had time to spend with her kids in the face of the ninety-hour week expectation for newly hired associates.

Rabbi Maderer, too, cited the lesson that it is okay to lie on account of peace in the household, and goes a step further. Here, the lie led to a change in lifestyle: Susan Pashman, the single mother, began a robust Shabbat observance her very first Friday night at home.[126] Rabbi Maderer sees the lie as a means for Pashman to move outside of her comfort zone and achieve something she secretly wanted—a respite from constant work demands. Or, put another way, I see the lie as concealing a greater truth. While she never observed Shabbat in the past, Pashman was telling a forward-looking truth. She took the opportunity to move her life in line with her "family first" values.

While I do not keep Shabbat myself, I am fascinated to see Pashman write that keeping Shabbat helped preserve her family, and even after her kids both left for college, Shabbat served as "a transfer point from the frenetic world of international banking to a world of reflective inwardness and peace."[127] On the day that Pashman told the "lie" about Sabbath observance, she made a calculated judgment call that is in line with Jewish teachings.

The Judgment of Truth

The Bible says that we should "execute the judgment of truth."[128] The scripture describes telling the truth to your neighbors and rendering sound judgments in the courts. In a similar way, Mussar teaches that, at the end of the day, we must use our own good judgment in deciding how much truth to reveal.

One way to execute the judgment of truth is by bringing together the soul traits of truth and loving-kindness. The Torah describes God

126 Pashman, "My Big Sabbath Lie—and the Joy It Brought."
127 Ibid.
128 Zechariah 8:16.

as abundant in truth and loving-kindness.[129] Scholars look at the jux-taposition of the two soul traits as a fusion concept, something greater than the sum of their respective parts.[130] The teaching suggests that we need to consider the consequences before we speak and to find the right balance between truth and kindness. As it says in Proverbs, "Do not let truth and loving-kindness leave you."[131] The following exam-ples strive to find right balance between absolute truth and a "lack of transparency" to spare another's feelings.

For example, say you learn that twenty years ago a friend's spouse had an affair. As far as you know, they are happily married today, with-out a whiff of infidelity since then. Should you tell the truth to your friend? Mussar suggests to me that the answer is no, for two reasons. First of all, this information would be hurtful and could damage their healthy relationship today. Second, this hearsay may not be factually correct. It may be uncomfortable for you to be in possession of this information, and the evil inclination may urge you to share the dis-comfort. But Mussar teaches that relieving personal discomfort is an insufficient reason for speech; we also need to consider the effect on other people. This is a particularly challenging example. While these types of situations don't come up often, they do come up. As we use our best judgment on how to act, we are enjoined to factor in kindness as well as truth when we are making a decision, and we are not sup-posed to say something simply to ease our own discomfort.

In Japan doctors sometimes do not tell a terminally sick person how ill they truly are.[132] The doctor perceives this as an act of kind-ness to spare the patient the upset and discomfort of knowing they are dying. In the United States this practice is generally looked down on, although there are circumstances when families choose not to tell a dying person the full truth of their condition. What do you think of

---

129 Exodus 34:6. The Orthodox Jewish Bible uses the phrase "abundant in Chesed and Emes," which are the Hebrew words for loving-kindness and truth.

130 *Parshablog*, "Is תֶמֱאֶו דֶסֶח a Hendiadys?"

131 Proverbs 3:3.

132 Kristof, "Tokyo Journal: When Doctor Won't Tell Cancer Patient the Truth."

this practice? Many people disagree with it and feel that in this case there is too much kindness, yet unless we are part of the family, know their full history, and live in their shoes, how are we to hold them in judgment?

In addition, executing the judgment of truth also reminds us to look at the truth from the perspective of everyone involved. For example, let's say that you and your mother have a challenging relationship. Every few years it flares up and ends in tears. Only God sits on the throne of truth, which means that your truth is no more valid than your mother's truth. Only when you understand your mother's truth to the core of your bones can you truly execute the judgment of truth. Ask yourself what a lifetime of hopes, fears, joys, and disappointments have done to your mother's soul. In the movie *Freaky Friday* a mother and teenage daughter switch bodies and have to live out a day as the other. They grow closer because they can truly understand what the other has been going through. Since we cannot actually live in another's shoes for a day, we must execute our best judgment of what that would be like.

Nine Types of Liars

In his thirteenth-century book *The Gates of Repentance*, Rabbi Yonah of Gerona listed nine categories of liars. It is instructive to review briefly.[133]

1. Outright liars who are completely untrustworthy

2. A con artist, i.e., one who pretends to be a friend in order to take advantage

3. People who use deception and misleading arguments to keep good things for themselves

4. Storytellers who embellish or outright lie to create a good story because they love doing it

---

133 Yonah of Gerona, *The Gates of Repentance*.

5. The type of person who makes a commitment with no intention of keeping it

6. Someone who intends to keep commitments but breaks them

7. A person who deceives others into thinking he has been helpful when, in fact, he hasn't been

8. Someone who claims virtues that she does not possess

9. The ninth type of liar doesn't lie as much as change things around when it suits them, more for satisfaction than to either achieve gain or cause harm

The point of the list is not to put someone else's name next to each category, although I'm sure some names popped into your head as you read it. (You'll learn why we shouldn't focus on the faults of others in the next chapter, Honor.) Our task in Mussar is to look within, to see how we have fallen into one or more of these categories at some point in our lives. You may even be feeling uncomfortable or defensive because one of these categories falls a bit too close to home. If this is you, rejoice! This means that you are approaching a powerful choice point and are thus empowered to make a healthy change in your soul.

Daily Practice

Mantra

"Be distant from falsehood" comes from the Torah; similarly, Exodus 23:7 says to "distance yourself from a false matter." As we have seen throughout the chapter, it is far easier to identify falsehood than it is to strive after an ideal of truth that is only available to the Divine. It is much easier to distance ourselves from falsehood than to strive for a shifting and complex canopy of truth.

Rabbi M. M. Levin offers a different mantra in his book *Chesbon HaNefesh* (*Accounting for the Soul*): "Do not allow anything to pass your lips that you are not certain is completely true."[134] This mantra provides a different strategy, to focus on remaining silent (chapter 14) rather than undertake the risk of speaking a falsehood.

Observe

According to the rabbis, people are untruthful for one of three reasons. As you go through your day, notice the times when you shade the truth and see which of these factors is in play.

Pursuit of permissible pleasures. There is something we want, and we think we can get it more easily if we are untruthful. For example, a child tells a parent that her room is clean and her homework is done so she can play a computer game. There are times when her parent discovers a pile of laundry in the room or the kid "remembers" later that night a math worksheet that is due the next day. Let's face it—each one of us has a little kid inside of us who would rather go play than do our homework. While the consequences of these lies may be small, they should be avoided because they can lead to a larger pattern of lying.

Pursuit of forbidden pleasures. In this case, the lie is to cover up for a pleasure that is taboo or unacceptable in some way, such as drug use or having an extramarital affair. I would also include in this category lies that are aimed at bolstering our own ego or standing in society, such as taking credit for another's work.

Fear of consequences. In this case, our lies are in response to fear about what will happen. For example, we are afraid of being judged by another person or afraid that we'll lose our job. Maybe we are afraid that we'll hurt someone's feelings if we tell the truth.

---

134 Levin, *Cheshbon HaNefesh*, 173.

Chapter 10

From My Journal

I really messed up by playing Candy Crush right before it was time to leave. I was almost an hour late picking up my daughter's friend to bring her to see my older daughter in a play. I really wanted to make up an excuse, but I was honest with the kids. I told them that I messed up: I was playing Candy Crush and lost track of time. I deleted the game from my iPad. Telling the truth prevented me from making an even bigger mistake by playing more in the future. Being late could have messed up my daughter's relationship with her friend. It was not great on my part. At least her friend knew it was my bad and not a reflection of my daughter's feelings.

Act

Whether we are untruthful because of fear or a desire for pleasure, untruth is an indication that another soul trait is out of balance. Here are a few ways to use soul traits we have already practiced to work on truth.

- **A humility imbalance could make you afraid that someone will judge you.** A humility imbalance could also lead to dishonesty if you erroneously think it is your job to decide that someone else can't handle the truth. By practicing humility, we could thus bring truth back into alignment. Try to take up less space by telling an uncomfortable truth. It isn't your place to decide what someone can or can't handle. Conversely, don't let fear of judgment allow you to cede your proper place.

- **Trust can help overcome fear of telling the truth, even a major fear like losing your job.** For example, you can remind yourself of your ability and trust that you can manage the negative reaction to telling the truth. We can also trust that we will be more respected and more authentic if we tell the inconvenient truth. In addition, we can trust that our family will support us whatever happens, and trust that God will be there to hold our hand and to help us get through it. What if telling the truth ultimately costs us our job? In that case, Mussar teaches that losing the job has a silver lining—e.g., that we would be spared pain, stress, and the potential legal exposure of working in an unethical environment.

- **Evaluate the truth tolerance at your employer.** Appetite for the truth can vary greatly from company to company. For example, I have a friend who worked for a local school district and was reprimanded for proactively disclosing an issue to parents that the district wanted to keep quiet. What is the culture of truth at your employer? Do you work for spin city or at a place where everyone is blunt to a fault? Develop a strategy for telling the truth with kindness.

- **When it comes to your career, however, be mindful that your truth may not be the only truth in play.** Is telling the truth merely giving an unpopular perspective or is it refuting a falsehood? Remember that you are expected to take the next step for you. It may be that distancing yourself from falsehood (below) may be more appropriate.

- **Practice patience to bear the burden of waiting for what you want until you can achieve it without shading the truth.** In fact, you may find that if you speak your truth without embellishment, you may end up getting what you want anyway, without the spiritual tint of guilt that can result from spin. Patience can also help us step away from a forbidden pleasure, as we get time to reflect, be grateful for what we have, and reconsider.

- **Distance yourself from falsehood.** While finding the truth can be difficult, detecting falsehood is much easier; often it just takes a good sniff. In your journal list three ways that you can distance yourself from falsehood. This may entail physically distancing yourself from certain people who are dishonest or maybe it means that you will no longer embellish stories. Pick one of the three, and carry it out for a week. Each night, write about your experiences in your Mussar journal.

- **Practice gratitude (chapter 12).** If we are grateful for what we have, we will not feel the need to go after what is forbidden.

Find the good in anyone.

Chapter Eleven
◆
Honor

Both humility and honor concern how we relate to other people. Humility focuses on knowing our proper place in the world. Honor focuses on the converse: giving others their due. Sometimes it can be hard to distinguish whether humility or honor is the soul trait being activated. In those cases I look at the issue through both a humility and an honor lens.

Assumption: We All Carry a Divine Spark That Is Occluded By Our Baggage

Every person, young or old, black or white, mean or kind, has a divine spark at the core of their being. This isn't a theory; it's a fact. (Well, actually, it's an assumption, but let's treat it as a fact and see where it takes us.) The meanest person you've ever met has a divine spark. The drug addict, the homeless, and the unfaithful spouse all have divine sparks that are hard for us to see.

No one was born mean. Have you ever seen a mean baby? Babies are cute and innocent. Somewhere along the way, things happen. We suffer hurts, humiliation, and disappointments, and thus develop baggage, i.e., pains that we carry with us that hold us back from being the best we can be. Our baggage keeps the divine spark from shining through. In addition, my baggage makes it hard for you to see my spark, and your baggage may obscure your spark from me.

One way to improve communication within a dysfunctional team is to have each person share the hardest thing they had to overcome in their childhood. Empirically, the exercise builds empathy and results in improved communication. On a spiritual level people are showing their baggage. When we see someone's baggage for what it is, we can't help but also see the divine spark shining through. Once we come face to face with another's divine spark, the way we interact with them is forever changed.

What an amazing thing it is to have a divine spark! When you think about it literally, if God walked in the room, would you treat God as you treat the people you interact with every day? Would you cut God off in traffic? Would you snicker about the clothes God chose for the day? I imagine that we would give God a free pass, or at least the benefit of the doubt, when it comes to these small interactions.

A friend shared with me an anecdote about a rabbi on a plane talking to his neighbor in the adjoining seat. As they were leaving the plane, the person said to the rabbi, "I don't need religion to find God. I can see God in a rainbow." The rabbi thought to himself, "Anyone can see God in a rainbow. The real trick is seeing God in the bum on the street."

Our task in Mussar is to learn to see God in the bum on the street. When we do, we'll no longer see him as a bum.

What Is Honor?

Mussar teaches that honor is the ability to recognize the humanity in other people, feel empathy, and treat them with respect, dignity, and even with reverence.

When you think about it, this is very different than the way we generally evaluate others. When we see someone, our normal response is to begin judging them—what they are wearing, how they talk, how smart they are, etc. It is easy to find fault with other people, in part because this can help us feel better about ourselves.

At the same time, we seem to have an insatiable hunger to be revered by other people. Mussar calls this tendency "chasing honor," a negative ego trip that damages our souls and relationships with other people. The only way to gain honor is by honoring other people; as Ben Zoma said in the Talmud, "Who has honor? One who honors others."[135]

Being Mindful of Judgments

We all tend to judge other people. Once, at a training workshop, my neighbor leaned over to me and said about the speaker, "He talks a good game, but he never followed through. I paid him a ton of money for his program, and when I emailed him I never heard back." She scowled with an indignant expression of bitterness and disappointment. A few minutes later the speaker shared a story with us—the previous year he had almost died from a viral infection. He put up pictures of himself in the hospital with tubes in his arm, down his throat, and up his nose. It was a shocking contrast to the lively and dynamic man before us. I heard my neighbor whisper, "My God, that was why he never got back to me." With tears in her eyes, she continued, "That is exactly during the time when I signed up for his program."

My friend was fortunate that she discovered the truth and no longer had to bear the anger and disappointment of her experience. Unfortunately, she had to go through months of pain and has to bear the guilt of spreading slander about the speaker.

There is wisdom in Rabbi Hillel's teaching to not judge another until you have stood in his place.[136] Note that my friend had every right to be disappointed and even angry that she did not receive the services that she purchased. I'm sure that many of us would have felt the same way in her situation. Where she went astray was when she created an

---

135 *Pirkei Avot* 4:1.
136 *Pirkei Avot* 2:4.

explanation in her mind for the speaker's behavior without knowing the facts, and then went on to form a judgment about his character based on the story she had created.

In his book *Every Day, Holy Day*, my Mussar teacher Alan Morinis includes "judging others favorably" as a separate soul trait.[137] For a daily mantra, he suggests this: "There's another side to the story." When you find yourself judging another, remind yourself that there is another side to the story.

As you practice honor, be mindful of how often you judge other people. How does it make you feel: angry because you feel wronged? Superior because you dress better than "that slob"? The words that pop into my head about others are not pretty; I would list them here but it is too embarrassing. Each time I judge other people, I am failing to honor their divine sparks.

The Spectrum of Honor

rudeness — too little — too much — flattery

What happens if we have too much honor? Too much honor leads to flattery and even obsequiousness. The flatterer is always praising other people, even when they don't deserve the praise. Excessive honor can lead to a form of manipulation by telling others exactly what they want to hear, even if it isn't true. Finally, when we honor others too much, we can neglect our own needs. For example, one of my coaching clients told me that she spent so much energy keeping her boss, her husband, and her kids happy that she didn't have anything left for herself.

Too little honor leads to rude and judgmental behavior. When we don't honor others, we are focusing too much on ourselves and on

---

137 Morinis, *Every Day, Holy Day*, 78–84.

our wants and our needs. Too little honor means not giving people the proverbial time of day or not looking them in the eye when they talk.

One of the dangers of success is that we may become inflated and, as a result, insufficiently honor others. For example, Rabbi Eleazar, son of Rabbi Simeon, was riding into a village, feeling happy about a recent accomplishment, when he was greeted by an old man. The rabbi, in his pride, said, "How ugly you are! Is everyone in this village as ugly as you are?"

The man replied, "Don't blame me for how I look; ask the Creator, who made me this way."

Rabbi Eleazar was abashed and immediately prostrated himself in apology.[138]

Rabbi Eleazar did not sufficiently honor the stranger. Although the rabbi was indeed better looking than the stranger, it did not give him the right to feel or act superior. As we saw in chapter 5, praise and success can strengthen the evil inclination, and in my opinion, that is exactly what happened here. Rabbi Eleazar's recent accomplishment strengthened his evil inclination and made him act in a boorish and cruel way. Later in the day, when the elation had passed, he may well have responded in a more appropriate way.

Flee from Honor

Mussar teaches that we should "flee from honor."[139] I was confused when I first read this. Why shouldn't we do honorable things, i.e., things that are good and can bring us praise? After all, it feels good to be praised by someone else, and why shouldn't we be recognized for our accomplishments?

One danger of being honored is illustrated by the story of Rabbi Eleazar that we just read. Praise can lead to a swelled head and arrogant behavior. In addition, the recognition can become more important

---

138 On1Foot.org provides a good translation and discussion of this story. Babylonian Talmud, Ta'anit 20A-B, http://www.on1foot.org/text/babyloniantalmud-taanit-20a-b.

139 Morinis, *Everyday Holiness*, 111.

to us than the accomplishment itself. When recognition becomes the primary driver, we start to chase honor. Because praise feels good, there is a natural tendency to chase honor, which is exactly why we are taught to flee from honor. When you start craving recognition, bring yourself back to the present moment.

My Honor Problem

I am someone who naturally craves honor, but I didn't realize it until years into my Mussar practice; I'll share with you how I found my keystone imbalance. While your spiritual curriculum is different, and honor may not be out of balance for you at all, you have a similar opportunity to find your keystone imbalance.

First, let me take you back to my time in the corporate world. I had never heard of Mussar, and my tool for self-investigation was the Enneagram personality classification system. Without going into detail on the Enneagram, I am a Type Three, the Performer/Achiever, which implies that my basic desire is to feel worthwhile, accepted, and desirable.[140] While I didn't realize it at the time, Type Three people are susceptible to chasing honor; this has served me poorly on many occasions.

For example, toward the end of my corporate career, my job was going well. My products were meeting their sales targets, issues were being resolved, and my opinion was sought after. Unfortunately, I had a habit of telling anyone who would listen that I was underutilized. I explained what a great manager I could be and that I wanted to be doing such-and-such instead of my current responsibilities. All I accomplished was to piss people off and set a high bar for myself. My manager told me that if I had just kept my mouth shut, everyone would have been very happy with my performance, but because I was chasing honor, they were nitpicking.

Five years later when I started to practice Mussar, I didn't realize that honor was even an issue for me. I thought that a humility imbal-

---

140 Riso and Hudson, *The Wisdom of the Enneagram*, 153.

ance was the root cause of my issues. I should have gotten a clue when I first came across this seminal teaching: "Who has honor? One who honors others."[141] When I first read this, I thought, "Huh?" It was like one of those cartoon computers going *Does not compute! Does not compute!* I am a doer, and the teaching suggests that honor does not come from doing. In my mind, I thought it should read, "Who has honor? One who makes their deliverables." To be honest, I just kind of blew it off and moved on. To be clear, Mussar teaches that taking action is important, but it is not okay to take action only for the sake of recognition.

The real shock came when I was taking my first Mussar class ("Everyday Holiness," an online class at the Mussar Institute). As part of the honor lesson, we were asked to praise three people a day. On the surface this should not be so hard to do, but for me it was incredibly hard; in fact, it seemed impossible. I would find myself praising the cats or a woman for her looks or clothes. I was amazed at how hard this was and couldn't wait for the two-week honor practice to be over.

As someone who prided himself as a doer, I was faced with a complete failure to perform a task. You know what? It was okay. Within the Mussar framework, I wrote in my journal and understood that I could learn from the process and that over time I would bring my honor toward balance. What is important is that I did make some small changes in my soul, and because I am on the lookout, I can often prevent my imbalance from making my life more difficult.

I don't think honor will ever be easy for me, but there are some hopeful signs. While writing this chapter I stopped by the grocery store. The woman behind the checkout was chatting with the customer in front of me about a movie. They were laughing and taking forever to put the half-dozen things she bought into a bag. I caught myself starting to feel irritable. To change the direction of my thinking, I focused on the fact that they were having fun, and I decided to take pleasure in their pleasure. When my turn came I decided to join in by asking the checkout woman what movie she recommended. I made myself notice

---

141 *Pirke Avos* 4:1.

---

the fun cowboy hat she was wearing. You know what? She was an old movie buff like I am! She made references to old movies, actors, and directors that this film reminded her of.

How cool is that? Mussar led me to a very human connection, and those thirty seconds made my day. I walked out of the store with a smile, grateful that God (or "the universe" for those of you uncomfortable with Divinity) brought me a wonderful opportunity to bring myself toward greater balance. I was grateful that I had taken advantage of the opportunity. Maybe honor isn't so hopeless for me after all.

Daily Practice

Mantra

The mantra for honor is "Find the good in anyone." Given our very human tendency to judge others, "find the good in anyone" offers an alternative. As you start to judge another, try to find the good in them. In fact, try to look for something good in every person you encounter during the day. What is the good in your annoying coworker? Maybe he dresses well. Maybe he speaks warmly about his children, even if he treats his admin poorly. Maybe she watches your favorite TV show. Finding the good in others is transformative because judging others is stressful. When you stop judging, you'll experience more calmness of the soul.

Observe

As you go through your day, pay attention to your impressions of other people. Observe how often you are judging them. Notice situations when you are chasing honor, in that you are craving attention or recognition. Pay attention to how you praise others; are you giving the right amount of honor or are you giving too much praise? Is the praise genuine and from the heart or is there a manipulative undercurrent to your words?

In addition, observe your internal world. When you are judging others, does it make you feel good? If you are praising others, does it make you feel bad?

Write about your observations in your journal at the end of the day or as they occur. Look for opportunities to act differently.

From My Journal

I was driving to the grocery store and was stopped at a red light. I looked at the driver of the car next to me. She was older, late-50s-plus, with a cigarette hanging out of her mouth. The first thought that popped into my head was "white trash." I needed to find the good, so I looked more closely at the car and I looked more closely at the driver. The car was immaculate. It was well cleaned, shiny, and overall it looked really nice. The driver must have gone to great lengths to make her car look so good. My whole judgmental attitude just melted away. I saw her as someone who fastidiously took great care of her car, who also happened to be smoking a cigarette.

Act

Pick one or two practices to help you influence your soul toward honor balance. Here are a few ideas to try.

- **Look for the divine spark in every person you meet.** Sometimes I find that it helps to squint, to bring them out of focus. The details become less sharp, and light and boundary blur. The person is still there but by altering the way we see them, we are given the opportunity to see through to the person inside. I am trying this right now as I write in Starbucks. The people start looking more and more similar, which means there is less for me to judge.

- **Look for the good when you notice yourself judging others.** See someone with uncombed hair? Notice that their clothes are clean. Dealing with a rude person? Notice a picture of their family on the desk.

- **Wear a rubber band around your wrist to remind yourself to look for the good.** When you find yourself judging, snap the rubber band.

- **Greet others before they greet you.** The Talmud teaches that Rabbi Yochanan Ben Zakkai made it a virtue to greet others in the marketplace before they greeted him, even gentiles.[142] You may want to crack a smile or roll your eyes that thousands of years ago, it was noteworthy that someone would honor people from outside his own community. Yet even today, when racism, tribalism, and unconscious bias are significant drivers of human behavior, someone who is blind to color and class is remarkable and praiseworthy; how much more so two thousand years ago!

  In accordance with this tradition, try to greet everyone before they greet you. A greeting may be a smile or it may also include a heartfelt hello. Be sure to greet people who are both different and less fortunate than you are. Try this for three days in a row, and record your experiences in your journal. How did it feel at the end of the day compared with the beginning of the day?

- **Eliminate one shaming behavior.** The book of Proverbs says, "One who disgraces his fellow is heartless."[143] In addition, according to sociologist Dr. Brené Brown, disgracing or shaming between couples "creates one of the dynamics most lethal to a relationship."[144] Shaming behavior is a sign that honor is out of balance. Think of a circumstance when your words shamed someone else. Maybe it was a child, a subordinate, or a peer. Resolve to eliminate one shaming behavior. Write the resolution in your journal. Include as much detail as you can about the circumstances that trigger this behavior in you, and keep track of your progress.

---

142 Berachos 17a, cited in Luzzatto, *Path of the Just*, 161.
143 Proverbs 11:12.
144 Brown, *Daring Greatly*, 104.

Give thanks for the good and the bad.

Chapter Twelve

◆

Gratitude

Many people find gratitude an easy soul trait to approach because they have heard of gratitude journaling. Research has shown that when you write down the things you are grateful for, it makes you happier.[145]

I had never kept a gratitude journal, but my knowledge of the practice encouraged me to start keeping my Mussar journal right away. Mussar takes gratitude to a different level. We give thanks not only for the good things that happen, but also for the bad things that happen. It was a new experience writing down bad things, then finding something to be grateful for.

Assumption: We All Share the Same Soul Traits and Have a Unique Measure of Each

Ever met a seemingly ungrateful person? Mussar teaches that an ungrateful person cannot exist. We all share the soul trait of gratitude. The so-called ungrateful person merely has a gratitude imbalance. This begs the question of what other traits are out of balance for

---

145 Tierney, "A Serving of Gratitude May Save the Day."

them, as often the soul trait imbalance we see on the surface is not the real issue. For example, perhaps the ungrateful person is insecure and never feels like they have enough. The insecurity itself stems from a humility imbalance.

Notice how differently you think of someone who is ungrateful and someone who is insecure. It becomes easier to treat the ungrateful person with kindness and compassion, as they must really be hurting inside.

There is not much we can do to help another on their spiritual journey. We can reassure insecure and ungrateful individuals that they are being taken care of and gently help them recognize the good in their life. But unless they are willing to do the work of addressing their own issues, insecurity and lack of gratitude will keep coming back. However, when we acknowledge that the other shares a trait with us, we see them in a new light, and we are transformed. Judgment becomes compassion and frustration morphs into peace as we become grateful that we are not so unhappy. Our frustration melts into a compassionate response. And maybe, just maybe, our compassion can give the other person an opportunity to see themselves in a new light too.

What Is Gratitude?

Mussar teaches that the gratitude soul trait governs our ability to recognize the good in any situation. In fact, the Hebrew word for this soul trait literally translates as "recognizing the good."[146] It is easy to get caught up in a litany of woe, listing all the injustices the universe has visited upon us. We lose sight of the fact that life itself is a gift. In fact, the terminally ill can seem to be more alive, filled with joy that they have survived to see another day. Mussar teaches us how to gain this appreciation while we remain alive and healthy.

In the Talmud, Ben Zoma teaches, "Who is rich? He who is happy with his lot."[147]

---

146 Morinis, *Everyday Holiness*, 64.
147 *Pirkei Avot (Ethics of the Fathers)* 4:1.

The ability to focus on the good things we have is an important element of practicing gratitude, but it isn't the only element. We are also enjoined to find the good in the bad things that happen to us. This means that if you break your leg, get a speeding ticket, or get dumped in a relationship, Mussar teaches that you should find the good in the situation. The good news is that finding the good in the bad is not as hard as it sounds.

The Spectrum of Gratitude

When we have too much gratitude we can become Pollyanna, remembering only the good and overlooking the bad, or we can become like Dr. Pangloss, a character in Voltaire's play *Candide*. Whenever tragedy happened Pangloss would say, "This is for the best in the best of all possible worlds."

The best of all possible worlds? If this were true, it would mean that nothing could possibly have happened other than this particular outcome. Such a thought is both disempowering and certainly untrue. If we are too grateful, we become complacent in the face of injustice or personal danger—and, in a sense, complicit in unjust situations. In short, too much gratitude stifles action and energy toward bringing about much-needed change.

Too little gratitude, on the other hand, can lead to depression. If we only focus on the negative and cannot appreciate the good things that are happening, we can become paralyzed by negative feelings. It is interesting that both too much and too little gratitude can lead to inaction. Alternatively, too little gratitude can lead to frantic busyness, a never-ending push to have more, more, and more. Recently I was stunned to see three people sitting in a hot tub on their cell phones.

One was playing a game, one was surfing, and one was on social media. Fear of missing out can drive this behavior, but what can you possibly be missing that is better than sitting in a hot tub? By being on your phone, you are missing out on a great experience *right now!*

Gratitude in balance also extends to objects in the physical world. For example, in the Torah Moses does not personally initiate the plague of blood against the Nile River; his brother Aaron initiates the plague by stretching his rod over the river.[148] The medieval French rabbi Rashi explained that because the Nile supported Moses as a baby (when his sister floated him downriver in a basket of reeds), Moses would not harm the river himself out of gratitude.[149]

Finding the Good in the Bad

Imagine that everything that happens in this world is for the good, meaning that even things that seem bad initially are really blessings in disguise. This was the attitude of a famous rabbi in the Talmud by the name of Nahum Ish Gamzu, who answered every unfortunate thing that happened to him with the phrase, "This too is for the good."[150] Rabbi Ish Gamzu was a man of great trust (chapter 8), so much so that he believed everything happened because it was part of God's plan, and since he trusted God, it must be "for the good."

In one story, Rabbi Nahum was given a chest of jewels to bring to Caesar to convince him to grant a petition from the Jews. He stopped at an inn where the innkeeper stole the jewels and refilled the chest with dust. When Caesar opened the chest he was enraged. As he was being dragged to prison, Rabbi Nahum said only, "This too is for the good."

Later that night, the prophet Elijah, disguised as one of Caesar's advisors, said to the emperor, "Surely the Jews would not deliberately

---

148 Exodus 7:19.
149 Rashi, commentary on Exodus 7, http://www.chabad.org/library/bible_cdo /aid/9868#showrashi=true.
150 Bialik and Ravnitsky, *Book of Legends*, 230–231:127.

insult Caesar in such a way. The dust must be magic. Send it with the army as they fight the troublesome barbarians."

Caesar did. Lo and behold, when Caesar's generals brought out the dust, the barbarians fled in terror and were defeated. Caesar gave Rabbi Nahum a chest of gold and jewels, granted his petition, and sent him home in honor. "This too is for the good," said Rabbi Nahum.[151]

The story offers an extreme example to illustrate a universal concept, the blessing in disguise, which we can employ in our everyday life. For example, if you get reprimanded at work, what is the good that can come out of it? Perhaps you learned that someone you trust is really a jerk. Maybe the reprimand today will prevent you from getting an even greater reprimand down the road. In fact, the reprimand might save your job if it lights a fire to learn a new skill you need to remain employed.

Grateful for a Layoff

Sometimes in life bad things happen.

When you are let go from a job you care about, what are some of the things you can be grateful for? You can be grateful for the connections you made, for the network you formed, for the skills that you learned and the money you made. You can be grateful for severance packages and a society that offers unemployment benefits. If you don't get a severance package, you can be grateful for the opportunity to reflect on what is truly important to you and to spend less money on things that don't make you happy. Being grateful also offers a plan of action. For example, when you are grateful for your network, you might remember a recruiter whom you spoke to recently or a former colleague who is now at a company you'd like to work for. Now you have two phone calls to make on the road to new employment.

Of course, sometimes life brings us things far worse than a layoff. In the face of trauma, chronic illness, or death, how is one to be grateful? Mussar teaches that we should look for something to be grateful

---

151 Ibid.

for even on the worst of days. Even if we've had the worst day we can imagine, we can still give thanks for being alive.

Why Gratitude Is Hard

Given the positive aspects of gratitude, why don't people practice gratitude more often? The Mussar classic *Duties of the Heart* gives three reasons why people do not feel gratitude:[152]

We become too absorbed in the worldly. When we are too focused on worldly things, we naturally gravitate toward wanting more. As a result, we quickly grow immune to the benefits we receive from the things we already have. What was a fancy car a year ago is now an older car.

We ignore the familiar and take it for granted. A former student of mine is a cancer survivor. At one point she was so sick that she could not get out of bed. As she recovered, she rediscovered the joy of everyday things. She shared that the first time she was able to use the on-ramp of the freeway was a particularly joyful milestone, in part because there was a time when she wondered if she would ever drive again. Let's stop and consider this point for a moment: *using an on-ramp was a source of joy.* How many of us drive every day? How often is the freeway a source of consternation and stress? Yet if we were no longer healthy enough to drive, how many of us would wish that we had enjoyed the driving while we had the ability?

When I was in my twenties I didn't understand why my grandfather was close to tears when he told me he was no longer allowed to drive. I was glad because I didn't think it was safe for him to drive. I was too young to appreciate what the loss must have felt like for him, and it certainly did not make me appreciate my youth and health any more. Mussar teaches

---

152 Morinis, *Everyday Holiness*, 67.

us to appreciate the good in the ordinary before it is taken away by old age or a health calamity.

We become preoccupied by the bad things. It is easy to be preoccupied by our latest setback or the person who is rude to us in the grocery store. At the same time, we forget about the twenty people who were not rude to us and the five people who smiled at us when we interacted with them.

Notice that each of these reasons derives from an unconscious behavior, which is a red flag that the evil inclination is at work. Gratitude helps us focus on the good things in our life, thus strengthening the good inclination.

Is the Glass Half Full or Half Empty?

This question is meant to remind us to focus on the good and the present as opposed to what is lacking, but this question never did it for me. Often people would bring it up when I was mad about something, and it seemed like an intellectual exercise that never helped me feel any better. One lesson from this experience is to practice gratitude for what you have when you are feeling calm, to prevent yourself from becoming angry about a "lack" of something.

In addition, I now understand that "half full or half empty" is not the right question. What if your glass is three-quarters full? Does that mean you should be happy? What if a few months ago the glass was 90 percent full? In that case, 75 percent full is not such a good situation. What if the glass is only a quarter full? Does that mean you should be unhappy or that you can't be happy? Maybe a year ago the glass was nearly empty. In this case, a quarter full is tremendous progress.

The reality is that the glass is always partly full and always partly empty. Mussar teaches us to be grateful for both the full and the empty. We should be grateful for what we have, if for no other reason than we could always have less. We can be grateful for the emptiness in the glass because, if nothing else, it helps us appreciate what we have and can spur us to change the situation.

Ben Zoma, a sage of the second century, expressed a similar sentiment when he wrote,

> What does a good guest say? *How much trouble my host goes through for me. How much meat he has offered. How much wine he has set before me. How many cakes he has brought before me. And all of this trouble he went through for me.* But an inconsiderate guest, what does he say? *What trouble has my host gone through? I have eaten one piece of bread and a single piece of meat. I have had but one cup of wine. All the trouble the host has gone to has been only for his family.*[153]

Think back for a moment on the soul trait of truth. Each guest has their own truth for the same meal. We have a choice for how we react to our circumstances. Do we feel grateful for what we have or do we wallow in self-pity about everything we don't have? There is no middle ground, for a lack of gratitude ultimately leads to self-pity.

Multiple Layers of Gratitude

Rabbi Yisroel Salanter, the founder of the nineteenth-century Mussar movement, shared a story of how he learned gratitude.[154] He once asked a café owner why his cup of coffee was so expensive. (In my mind he says with a Yiddish accent, "So much for beans and water?")

The owner explained, "I am not just selling you beans and water. You also have this nice atmosphere and friendly service. The coffee is made and brought to you, and you have a nice table to sit at with a nice window to look outside."

Rabbi Salanter realized that he was only seeing but a small portion of everything it took to create his coffee. In a similar way, so much effort goes into making the world the way it is. When we turn on a light switch we should be grateful for the thousands of people who helped make it happen. They built and maintained the electrical network, mined the fuel for the generators, manufactured the light bulb, transported it to the store, and, for that matter, sold it to us. Without all of their collective efforts, we would sit in the darkness every night.

---

153   Berachos 58a, 681:373 Book of Legends.
154   L'Neshama, "Rav Yisroel Salanter's Expensive Cup of Coffee."

In a similar way, when we begin to become too proud of our accomplishments, we should remember to be grateful to all of the people who made our successes possible. Could we have accomplished them without the government that provides infrastructure and safety, the teachers who educate us, the family that supports us, or the people who remove the trash? It is hard for me to imagine a successful artist or businessman having to labor surrounded by heaps of smelly rubbish.

In that light, let me take a moment to thank every barista within ten miles of my home in San Carlos. Given how much of this book was written in Peets, Starbucks, or Philz, I don't know what I would have done without the wonderful coffee, free Wi-Fi, and friendly atmosphere.

Daily Practice

Mantra

"Give thanks for the good and the bad." In the Mussar context, gratitude is not only about being thankful for the good things that happen. We also look for the good in anything bad that happens and then give thanks for it. I explained this concept to my father. At first he was skeptical, and then he remembered how in 1962 he flunked out of navigator training in the air force and initially was devastated. Had he passed, however, he would have remained in the air force and been sent to Vietnam. The Vietnam War also gave him something to be thankful for: to build support for the war, Congress expanded eligibility of the GI Bill, so he could go back to college. Thus, even devastating personal setbacks and calamities like Vietnam opened the door for something good to happen.

Observe

Earlier in the chapter I shared the Mussar teaching that lack of gratitude arises from being too absorbed by the worldly, taking the good for granted, or becoming preoccupied by the bad. As you go through your day, be mindful of these tendencies and be sure to record your observations in your journal at night. Within a week, you will start to notice tendencies. For example, you might notice that you become pre-occupied by negative events. Alternatively, you might notice that you never acknowledge the good in your life.

Pay particular attention to your interactions with the people you care most about. How are you expressing your gratitude toward them? Do you call your parents or greet your spouse with a big smile each night?

Entry 1: Being cold in the woods reminded me that today our survival is so easy. If we needed to worry about food and shelter, we wouldn't even notice the small things that get under our skin.

Entry 2: It was hard for me to cultivate an attitude of gratitude about the volunteering situation. Why? I was offered a place on a different committee, and the people were welcoming and friendly. Getting kicked off that one committee, this too is for the good. Is that hard for me to accept because of my ego? Am I worried about what others will think? I am really stressed about the event coming up when everyone from the old committee will be there too.

Act

As your gratitude practice begins, take a few minutes to write down all of the things that you are grateful for. Can you keep writing for five minutes?

Now pick one area of your life where you would like to experience more gratitude, and set an intention to take action. Complete this sentence:

- I will bring more gratitude into my life by
_____.

Gratitude

If you are at the other end of the spectrum, finish this sentence:

- I need to be less grateful because _____.

- Therefore, I will _____.

Here are some additional suggestions for your gratitude practice:

- **Write in your journal the experiences from the day that touch upon gratitude.** Include the things that made you happy as well as things that went badly. For each negative, look for a silver lining.

- **Write down three of the worst things that ever happened to you.** What is the good that came out of them?

- **Bring gratitude to every life situation as a means to combat impatience or frustration.** For example, if you are stuck in traffic, focus on being grateful that you are still healthy enough to drive. Annoyed with a coworker? Find a way to show your appreciation to someone you have taken for granted at work.

- **Show the people in your life *more* gratitude *every* day.**

- **Practice humility or honor if you tend to show too much gratitude.** The excessive gratitude may be arising from another soul trait out of balance, such as humility or honor. Pick a humility or honor practice to help bring gratitude into balance. Over dinner, share the best things that happened during the day before talking about the negative.

First things first and last things later.

Chapter Thirteen

◆

Order

My first thoughts on practicing order? "Oy, this is going to be rough." I was so messy in college that I converted my sophomore-year roommate from an ultra-neat individual to someone who left piles of clothes on the floor. In reality, practicing order wasn't nearly as bad as I feared it would be. The fear was merely preemptive resistance from the evil inclination. The discipline of Mussar practice helped me to "just do it" without becoming paralyzed.

Assumption: We All Carry a Divine Spark That Is Occluded By Our Baggage

It might surprise you that I'm beginning the chapter on order with the assumption about the divine spark, especially given that order governs the laws of nature. I do not understand why so many people create the false dichotomy between faith and science. There are many reasons to have doubts about Divinity, but science should not be one of them. I have a PhD from MIT in biology. I see divine handiwork everywhere—in the elegant ways that cells grow and divide, the incredibly regular structure of DNA, and beautiful array of colors and patterns within a leaf. At the highest level, both faith and science are about ideas and philosophy.

The Shema prayer, which holds a special place in Judaism, is instructive. It says, "Hear O Israel, the Lord is our God, the Lord is One." "The Lord is One" affirms that God is a part of everything, that we are all connected to each other and to all parts of creation. Author Eckhart Tolle makes a similar point when he refers to the illusion that we are all separate; by acknowledging the oneness of all, we can become enlightened—more complete and compassionate people.[155] The divine spark is that element of oneness that resides within, and it shows through when we let it.

Judaism teaches that when we are building or making something, we are assisting God in the act of creation.[156] At the same time, we need to remember that God also created the laws of entropy, where things tend to get messier. So God does not intend for things to be too orderly. If you aren't sure about Divinity, the reality of the spectrum from order to chaos is self-evident.

What Is Order?

Order is the soul trait that gives structure to our lives. For example, order governs if and how we plan, how often we put away our things, and how we react if we walk into a messy room. Although it has taken me years, I now understand that some people actually get physical stress symptoms when they walk into a messy room or chaotic environment. In fact, as my order soul trait has come toward balance, I sometimes feel this too. Order also governs the laws of physics and is critical for the proper functioning of everything from machines to plants and animals.

The Hebrew word for order is *seder*, the same word we have for the traditional Passover meal. The Passover seder is all about doing things the same way year after year. We have a guidebook, the Haggadah,

---

155 Tolle, *The Power of Now*, Kindle edition, 11–12.
156 Marder, "The Call: Erev Rosh Hashana 5773."

which guides us through the stories, songs, and practices. *Haggadah* is translated as "the telling," and we tell the story of the Israelites' exodus from Egypt and out of slavery year after year.

The Spectrum of Order

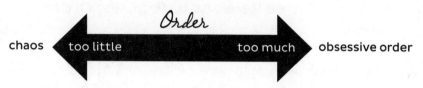

Mussar teaches that when we have too much order we get obsessive, the most extreme form of which is akin to obsessive-compulsive disorder. Obsessive order limits freedom, as one feels compelled to put everything in exactly the right place and to try making things happen at the right time. It is very stressful to live trying to control the outcome of everything. Things change all the time in this world, and Mussar teaches that by fighting change, we are fighting the Divine Will for the universe.

Whether or not you believe in Divinity, the reality is that most things are completely outside of your control. We can choose to either align with or fight the direction things are going. When we align with the direction things are going, we are aligning with the will of the universe.

Of course, just blindly accepting whatever direction things are going is to swing to the side of too little order. Too little order leads to chaos and disarray. As I wrote earlier, order is a challenge for me. I've wasted far too much of my life looking for things that I misplaced. Just the other day I almost had a meltdown because I could not find a check my mother had sent my daughters as a gift. Had I been more orderly and taken care of the check right away, I would have saved myself a lot of unnecessary pain.

Order in balance relies on routines to create structure without conscious thought, which in turn saves stress and time. For example, when I unload the dishwasher before I eat breakfast, the rest of the day goes much better. My family can load the dirty dishes as we use them, which makes the evening go by much more smoothly. It seems like whenever I don't unload in the morning, at 9 PM I need to unload and then deal with a kitchen full of dirty dishes.

Three Reasons to Practice Order

Rabbi Eliyahu Dessler was a teacher of Mussar in the early part of the twentieth century. He taught that order was a keystone soul trait. Dessler and his students were immaculately dressed because he felt that external order promoted an orderly mind.[157] Rabbi Dessler gave three reasons why practicing order is important:[158]

Practicing order gives inner satisfaction and confidence. When you are put together well, when you know where things are and when things are proceeding on a predictable schedule, life is less stressful, which allows you to go about the tasks you need to do with confidence.

Order helps you find things and saves time. I once toured a manufacturing plant and was amazed at how structured and orderly everything was. For example, the tools drawer had an outline of each tool on the bottom, so you knew exactly where to put the tool when you were done with it. And when you needed a tool, you knew exactly where to find it.

Some things, like a clock, only function properly when everything is ordered properly. As our society becomes more complicated and dependent on technology, order is more important than ever. Our society has a complicated energy distribution system, and we live in an international economy. Something can go wrong in another part that affects us directly. Many things need to function properly for these systems to hold together.

---

157 Morinis, *Everyday Holiness*, 88.
158 Ibid., 11.

Disorder within Order

In the biblical book of Numbers, God gives Moses elaborate instructions specifying where each tribe should camp. For example, the tribe of Judah was instructed to camp to the east, the tribe of Issachar next to the tribe of Zebulun, and so on. Moreover, God instructed that the tribes should march in this same order.[159]

Why would God go to the trouble of specifying the marching order and placement of each tribe's tents? As context, the Israelites were newly liberated from slavery in Egypt and had fallen into whining and grumbling about their living situation. According to the Torah, there were 600,000 men in the exodus; imagine the chaotic scrum of competing tribes without a defined order to march in. If Moses tried to specify the marching order and sleeping arrangements on his authority alone, there would have been arguments and more dissent. Because God specified the order, there was no argument and the people could focus on more important issues.

At the same time, within their designated camping location, each tribe could arrange the tents as it wished. When the non-Jewish prophet Balaam saw the Israelite encampment, instead of cursing the Israelites, he gave the following blessing: "How fair are your tents, O Jacob, your dwellings, O Israel."[160] Balaam was moved by the arrangement of tents that were clearly clustered together but offset so the entrances did not line up, giving each family privacy.

Thus, there were three levels of organization: the overall encampment, areas for each tribe, and then the arrangement of the individual tents. Today we can see similar levels of hierarchy, where membership in a larger group can come in different flavors. For example, a corporation has different departments, and each department may have its own seating arrangement. Some may have cubes and others open tables. The people within each of these departments will have their own culture and their own way of interacting with each other, yet they are part of a larger whole.

---

159 Numbers 2:1–9.
160 Numbers 24:5.

Rabbi Shefa Gold sees this passage in Numbers as a metaphor for the chorus of different voices within our brain.[161] She notes that the placement of the tribes at the different points of the compass carries implications about the choices we face every day. For example, the tribes to the east "face the rising sun, opening to new beginnings, new possibilities." The tribes to the south bask in "warmth, comfort, and consistency." Rabbi Gold teaches that when we are faced with a spiritual challenge there is a conflict between these different approaches, and we need self-compassion, patience, and humor to figure out the right course of action.[162]

In addition, order can help us resolve the conflict between the voices. Each voice is speaking to a different set of priorities. It is the task of order to set priorities in line with our values and the situation. For example, let's say that you need to decide whether to leave a secure job at a large company for a more exciting opportunity at a start-up. Order not only helps you evaluate the risk/reward trade-offs of each option, it also can help you devise an appropriate transition plan.

Order at the Start-Up Versus a Large Corporation

The appropriate level of order is situation dependent. Let's look at the difference between a start-up and a corporation. A mature company needs to have processes and procedures. It may have regulatory requirements for meticulous paperwork and written approvals in order to make changes to the manufacturing process. When people are buying from a large company they expect a consistent level of quality, which requires a tighter structure.

A start-up, on the other hand, would go out of business if it had that much structure. The key issue is to get something out the door as quickly as possible. Customers are far more tolerant of bugs and issues

---

161 Gold, *Torah Journeys*, 137.
162 Ibid.

because they are using something new and untried. A start-up is constantly improvising and tinkering to get its innovative product to work.

Imagine what would happen if you tried to get rid of all the procedures at big companies. I don't have to imagine—I've seen it happen, and it is *ugly*! Chaos ensues as factions struggle for power because there is no logical or systematic plan to allocate resources and priorities.

In fact, I have seen a lack of order absolutely ruin a product's potential in the marketplace. One of the largest companies in the biotech field bought a start-up with a promising technology. They set an aggressive launch deadline and put lots of resources toward making the date. When they fell behind and a powerful competitor emerged, the general manager was given a blank check for anything the team needed, and then they got rid of all process. People would come up to me in the hall, gleefully saying things like, "Greg, it is so wonderful. We don't need to waste time with all these checkpoints! Now we can just get it done." I would nod politely and thank my lucky stars that I was not on the project.

The glee those team members felt was from the evil inclination run amok. The frenetic energy was masking their judgment. Big, complicated projects require planning, and checkpoints are a mechanism to make sure the team has thought through the key issues and planned to account for risks. They made the launch date and shipped a half-million-dollar instrument to dozens of customer sites. Care to guess how things turned out?

The instruments did not work, and the problems with them were all different! Talk about a nightmare to support. The company spent millions handholding customers to get them up and limping, which drained the resources needed to fix the root cause issues. A start-up with one or two customers easily could have managed the situation, but a market leader trying to make this product work for dozens of customers was a disaster. The product was pulled from the market a few years later.

This example illustrates the power of the evil inclination. The late Rabbi Alan Lew[163] called the evil inclination "the tumultuous whirlwind of impulses and dysfunctions that prevents us from doing what we should be doing."[164] Were Rabbi Lew to listen to this example, I think he would say that there is no blame in the situation. Sometimes we are helpless before our impulses. Here, the lure of "just getting it done" was too seductive, given the tight deadline.[165] Fortunately, Rabbi Lew provides a solution: we can strengthen the good inclination through spiritual work, meditation, and acts of loving-kindness such that, over time, we become better able to resist the seductive and seditious voice of the evil inclination.[166]

Daily Practice

Mantra

The mantra for order is "First things first and last things later."[167] As with all soul traits, there are other mantras to choose from. In his book *Everyday Holiness*, Alan Morinis offers the following: "Order creates inner alignment, peaceful and prepared."[168] Whatever mantra you choose to begin your day, it should be something that resonates for you and helps frame your day for you to notice your soul trait of order in action.

Write the mantra on an index card and place it on your bedside table or on the bathroom mirror where you will see it in the morning. Take a few minutes to chant it to yourself in order to prepare for your day.

---

163 Rabbi Lew was former rabbi of mine. He is dearly missed in the community.

164 Lew, *This Is Real*, Kindle edition, 201.

165 As a recovering workaholic, I can testify that there is nothing like the adrenaline rush of frantic product development.

166 Ibid.

167 *Pirkei Avot* 5:10

168 Morinis, *Everyday Holiness*, 87.

Observe

As you go through your day, be on the lookout for times when order is affecting your inner and outer worlds. The habit of self-observation may help you notice when some of the previous soul traits have been activated. For example, although this week I'm focusing on a different soul trait, I can see that disorder is on the rise. I have been losing things and forgetting appointments, and I haven't been unloading the dishes in the morning. As a result, I am experiencing more stress at night.

Remember that sometimes the best way to balance one soul trait is by practicing another. Often a lack of external order is a result of an underlying humility imbalance. We enjoy a pleasure like having a drink in the TV room but are unwilling to take responsibility for cleaning up. Alternatively, we could be imposing our rigid cleanliness standards because we are not patient enough to wait for others to clean up later. Therefore, working on humility or patience may be the appropriate way to bring order into balance.

Write in your journal at night about your tests during the day that relate to order. Writing is itself an important exercise of order. It is not sufficient to simply think about the day. Writing makes it more concrete and easier to notice patterns day-to-day.

From My Journal

Entry 1: I swept the sidewalk today to get rid of the fallen leaves and unloaded the dishwasher early. My bedtime routine was faster tonight until I couldn't find my pajama bottoms. I finally found them in my laundry bag—this morning I must not have been in the moment.

Entry 2: Got my daughter to practice on time. I did well reaching out to a parent I know from another season to pick her up.

Act

Sometimes journaling can help you pick an intention for a soul trait. After two weeks of focusing on order, night after night I was writing about my pajamas. Most nights I would spend thirty seconds searching the bedroom and bathroom looking for them. It was stressful and frustrating. I decided to practice order by putting my pajamas under my pillow every morning. It took away a significant source of stress and has made no discernible effect on my morning schedule. I shared this practice with one of my Mussar teachers, who said it was a great idea. She also invited me to remember my divine spark, asking, "Would God really leave his pajamas on the ground?" I don't anymore!

Here are a few ideas to help you practice order:

- **Ask yourself where you sit on the spectrum of order.** Are you leaning toward the chaos side or more toward the extreme order side? Think about one area or opportunity in your life affected by your order soul trait. What is one small step that you can take toward balance?

- **Practice trust by letting go of a situation if you are on the more structured side.** For example, when someone makes a suggestion, instead of trying to correct them to optimize the outcome, just let them decide and live with the uncertainty, trusting that things will turn out okay.

- **If you lean more toward the chaotic side, pick one small area where you can bring more order.** For example, you could:

  - Bring your dishes from the table to the kitchen and/or load the dishwasher right after you leave the table.

  - Find a regular place to put your computer every night instead of dropping it in a random location in the living room.

  - Create a to-do list every morning.

- **Take a baby step toward order through partial cleanups.** If you are the kind of person who leaves coffee cups or glasses in the living room, try bringing them toward the kitchen. Ideally, you would put them in the dishwasher when you were finished, but that may be too big a step for you to take. Instead, what if you walk toward the kitchen when you get up and put the dish down somewhere along the way? This may not satisfy your fastidious housemate who is always on you to "clean up your junk," but it does satisfy your Mussar practice because you will have taken a step from where you are to where you want to go.

- **Planning is a powerful way to practice order.** Set some time aside to plan your day and your week.

- **Leave something out of place if you are super fastidious.** For example, leave one dirty dish on the table all day. What happens inside you? What soul trait becomes activated? Write about it in your journal.

Nothing is better than silence.

Chapter Fourteen

◆

Silence

I am a talker. I said my first word at ten months old, and the family joke is that I haven't stopped talking since. In first grade I had to stay after school almost every day for talking in class. I continued to talk in class through graduate school, and I still like to talk a lot. I first approached the soul trait of silence with trepidation because it does not come naturally to me. It feels more authentic to share my thoughts as I have them.

Assumption: We Are Driven By a Conflict Between Good Inclination and Evil Inclination

How does this relate to silence? Silence governs speech, focusing on when we should talk and when we should remain silent. When we are upset, the evil inclination gains ascendancy and we speak without restraint, saying words that we would never say when calm. The more upset we get, the greater the power of the evil inclination to damage our relationships in a lasting way.

In his book *Words That Hurt, Words That Heal*, Rabbi Joseph Telushkin teaches that we should "fight fair," which means only arguing about the immediate issues, and "never use damaging personal information to invalidate your adversary's contentions."[169] When we bring up past transgressions in an argument, we escalate to a hurtful and destructive fight that can damage a relationship forever. To illustrate the point, Rabbi Telushkin points to the severed relationship between King David and his first wife, Michal, who was the daughter of the previous king, Saul.[170]

What had been a loving relationship that survived war, assassination attempts, other lovers, and a war between David and Michal's father was lost over ill-spoken words. When David was returning to Jerusalem in triumph, he danced with elation in the streets, which Michal viewed with "contempt" from her window. When David arrived at home, presumably expecting a congratulatory greeting, he was met instead with scorn. She spoke sarcastically to him for "exposing himself before his servants' slave girls like some vulgar exhibitionist!"[171] David responded by going for the jugular, bringing up the most hurtful thing in her past when he reminded her that God "chose me over your father and over everyone in his family to make me chief." The story ends with David going to spend the night with the slave girls, the implication being that David and Michal were never lovers again.[172] Both David and Michal were overtaken by their respective evil inclinations, which led them to pronounce hurtful words that put a loving relationship forever out of reach.

We too are susceptible to the danger of saying things that we regret later if we allow our evil inclination to become too strong. The more emotional or upset we get, the harder it is to calm down, and the harder it is to keep our tongue in check.

Mussar teaches us that the evil inclination needs to be guided by the good inclination. We cannot and should not want to get rid of the evil inclination. It is part of who we are, and emotion can be a key driver for

---

169 Telushkin, *Words That Hurt*, 87.

170 Ibid., 70–71.

171 2 Samuel 6:20, *Complete Jewish Bible*.

172 Telushkin, *Words That Hurt*, 71.

good. By practicing meditation and living mindfully, we can strengthen the good inclination, which in turn may give us the strength to wait before we speak. Even an extra second can be enough to forestall angry words that can lead to a lifetime of regret.

What Is Silence?

Silence is the trait that governs when we talk and when we do not. Mussar teaches that silence also opens a space for God to come into our lives. When we are always on the go, with constant sounds like the radio in the background, we will not be able to hear the quiet whispers from our soul. If you are not sure of Divinity, think about how many times you have an inspiration when in the shower or just relaxing.

The primary consideration for speaking is not what our intent is; it is about what effect our speech has on other people. This relates to our prior practice of truth. We do not speak the truth if our words will only hurt other people without any other good outcome.

Silence is what mediates the difference between music and noise. Music is different notes—sounds at different frequencies with spaces in between. Music has regularity, a rhythm that is distinct from the noise of a leaf blower or traffic. Without the spaces, we would not have music. Our speech should be like music and bring beauty and light to the world.

The Spectrum of Silence

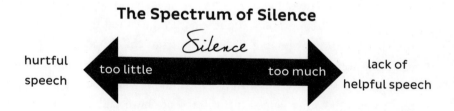

Silence

hurtful speech

too little

too much

lack of helpful speech

Rabbi Alan Lew reminds us that speaking has the power to bring things into existence,[173] as it is written, "God said, 'Let there be light'; and there was light."[174] In a similar way, our speech has tremendous power to bring light to the world. When there is too little silence we are losing an opportunity to bring good into existence. This includes not only kind words, but also the normal communication of everyday cooperation at work. Speech also is a critical prerequisite for repentance; in order to be forgiven, we need to ask for forgiveness. In order to receive pardon from God on Yom Kippur, we need to speak our sins aloud. Without speaking our sins, they remain trapped within, where they can grow and take on a life of their own. It is like the old saying "the truth will set you free." The statement implicitly suggests that the truth must be spoken for this anodyne to be actualized.

In addition, there are times when we are not only expected to speak, we are required to speak out. For example, if there is a fire, we are expected to call the fire department. If a physician sees evidence of child abuse, they are required to call the police and social services. Not only is speaking out against injustice the law, it is a core Jewish value. It is not good enough to do no evil; we are also expected to be proactive to prevent bad things from happening.

Too little silence, on the other hand, produces hurtful speech. Judaism teaches that the bar is very high for when we are supposed to speak; we are only supposed to speak when we can bring some good into the world. The obligation is on the speaker not to offend. Good intentions don't count, only the results, as measured by the effect of the speech on other people. The lesson from childhood that "if you can't say something nice, don't say anything at all" does not go far enough. The Mussar version would add "and if what you say inadvertently hurts the other person, you should not have said it."

Unfortunately, I was born with no filter between what I think and what I say. When I was very young I thought my grandmother smelled funny, and I told her so. To this day, more than forty years later, I still

---

173 Lew, *This Is Real*, 198.
174 Genesis 1:3.

remember the look of hurt on her face. I feel the pain and guilt, and now that she is gone, I cannot apologize. Maybe writing this will set me free of those guilty feelings.

We all love to have our say, but frankly, this should not be a consideration. A student told me the best career advice she was ever given was to stay quiet in meetings unless you have something to say that can help move things forward. When she shared her experience with the group, I felt uncomfortable because I like to speak off the cuff. Sometimes some really interesting things come out of my mouth. Well, they are interesting to me. It was painful to think that perhaps speaking off the cuff wasn't a helpful or good strategy, and I remembered some awkward exchanges in business meetings where this had been clearly the case. I had been speaking because I liked to talk, and I get energy from verbal exchanges. The "me me me" attitude suggests that for me, speaking off the cuff is rooted in a humility issue. Silence teaches that before we speak, we need to think "you you you."

Avoiding Hurtful Speech

The implications of silence are profound. How often do we take the role of the judge, saying something we think someone needs to hear or delivering a message "for their own good"? Who are we to decide what they need to hear? How often is "for their own good" simply a rationalization for exacting a bit of verbal revenge for a hurt or slight we are feeling? When I hear a student (or myself) say something negative about another person, I ask them (or myself), "Where is that thought coming from, the evil inclination or the good inclination?" The evil inclination can take the form of righteous indignation or a cry for justice. It is not our place to be judge, jury, and verbal executioner. More often than not, it is the evil inclination that is driving the question. When that is the case, my rule is to try to stay silent.

Sometimes hurtful speech can have a more innocuous origin. Many a backseat driver means no harm and is acting from their own nervousness, yet some people find comments about driving very annoying.

Even if meant well, such comments should not be said if the person doesn't want to hear them.

Harmful Speech Kills Three People

The Talmud teaches that harmful speech kills three people: the one who is speaking, the one being spoken about, and the one who is listening.[175] While the damage to the one being spoken about is self-evident, the damage to the speaker and listener are worth exploring. Psychiatrist Antonio Wood teaches that when we speak ill of someone, we alienate ourselves from them psychologically, and the more people we become alienated from, the greater our risk for depression.[176] Conversely, Rabbi Telushkin writes that people who avoid harmful speech find their connections to other people "more intimate and satisfying" because speakers are forced to focus more on themselves and the people they are speaking to.[177]

"Killing the one who is listening" means that we are not supposed to listen to gossip. It is natural to enjoy stories about people, especially when they are salacious or unusual.

"So-and-so is having an affair."

"Sandra made an idiot out of herself in the meeting."

"The real reason why he quit was because he felt unappreciated."

If you hear that someone did something unethical, your opinion of them may forever be affected, even if you later hear that it wasn't true. You can tell yourself not to be judgmental, but some part of your brain will always wonder which account was true and which was false. For this reason gossip kills the listener; as Mussar practitioners, we are enjoined to avoid listening to gossip.

Damning with faint praise is an insidious form of gossip that is prevalent in the corporate world. For example, I interviewed a middle manager who told me that a good friend of his had used this trick to betray him. He and a colleague were both up for a promotion. She

---

175 Talmud Arachin 15b.
176 Telushkin, *Words That Hurt*, 5.
177 Ibid.

got it. Initially he thought that they were buddies and had no hard feelings. Then he learned his colleague was going around saying, "Jack is really good, he's great, but he has a tendency to _____." By first praising him, it set people off their guard. Then she mentioned just this tiny fatal flaw. That spread enough doubt about him that he was not promoted.[178]

Once again, we are enjoined to avoid harmful speech. In this case, we need to try not to listen to such backhanded comments by finding a way to redirect the conversation. Otherwise we may hear something that is untrue, and there is no way to erase it from our memory.

Feathers in a Pillow

There is a Jewish story told in various forms about the dangers of gossip.[179] A man who loved to tell tales shared a weird story about someone in town. It got back to the man, who went to the rabbi, distraught because his business was ruined. The rabbi called in the storyteller and asked him to stop spreading the story.

"But it's true," he explained.

"True, not true, what does it matter? You've killed this man's reputation."

The man was sorry, as he did not think spreading this tale could have such a bad effect.

"What can I do?" he asked.

The rabbi instructed him to rip open a down pillow and scatter the feathers. Then he told him to take all the feathers and put them back inside the pillow. "That is impossible," cried the man. "The wind has blown the feathers everywhere."

The rabbi explained that this is exactly why gossip is such an evil. Once false or harmful speech gets out there, it is impossible to ever bring it back. At the rabbi's instruction, the man apologized to every person he had told the story to, explaining the evils of harmful speech.

---

178 Marcus, *Busting Your Corporate Idol*, 67–68.
179 Brombacher, "A Pillow Full of Feathers."

Silence of the Mind

Silence is also a soul trait that governs the mind. Our head can be filled with thoughts jumping from one place to another, making it hard for us to focus on anything. Rabbi Nachman of Breslov taught, "You are wherever your thoughts are. Make sure your thoughts are where you want to be."

Practicing silence externally can help quiet our mind internally. I had a student who practiced silence by turning off her car radio when she was driving home. One warm and sunny day, she turned off the radio and rolled down the windows of her car. Soon she started to hear things she had never heard before: the leaves under the tires, birds singing, the wind in the trees. She found herself experiencing a connection to the world that would have been impossible with the radio blaring and the windows up.

Daily Practice

Mantra

"Nothing is better than silence."

As it says in the book of Proverbs, "In abundance of words, offense will not be lacking, but one who restrains his lips is wise."[180]

Observe

As you go through your day, pay attention to what you say and do not say. If you are like me, then talking too much will get you into trouble. However, you may be the kind of person who often wishes that you'd said more. Whether you are outspoken or not, you may be plagued by rumination, replays of conversations in your head, wishing they had gone differently.

In addition, pay attention to what other people are saying. How often is it gossip? How does it make you feel when you hear gossip? Does a part of you enjoy hearing that a rival got shot down in a meeting? Do you feel important because you are in the know about a juicy

---

180 Proverbs 10:19.

tidbit that isn't widely known? What other soul traits are being activated for you?

Write down your observations each night in your journal.

From My Journal

Entry 1: I got too fired up today because of the real high traffic to my blog. Someone wrote a blog post on another website about being sane in an insane work situation. I referred to her on Twitter as "the sanity queen," which got me called an ass. I got really upset because I meant it as praise. When I am honest with myself, I realize that I wanted attention but by being clever and trying to be witty, I got called an ass. If I had been silent, the stress I am feeling would have been avoided. I realize I had lost my equanimity. I got too high from my success, which led me to speak too much, and then I ended up feeling down.

Entry 2: Today I was yelling at the kids from the sideline during the soccer game. I felt really bad about it afterwards. It was not healthy speech. Coaches do not yell during games, the kids do not hear it, and it can only fluster them or hurt. I am embarrassed that I did not follow silence. I was much better the second game, and I enjoyed it a lot more just cheering.

Entry 3: We had a nice end-of-year party for the committee I volunteer for. If I had not had the big fight on the other committee, I never would have made it to this team that is a better fit for me. We raised more money than the previous year and were recognized for it. I was not leading and I feel like we would not have made the goal if I were. Maybe that is an overreaction. I need to trust that things worked out for the best, and would have whatever my role on the committee, and follow silence in my head. I did not talk much during the party; I wish I had engaged more. On the positive side, although I was frustrated about people being late, I did not make any snarky comments to the latecomers.

Act

As you go through your next two weeks practicing silence, here are a few things to try.

- **Listen more than you talk if you are a talker.** Before you speak, take the advice of Rabbi Levin, author of *Accounting of the Soul*. He teaches before speaking that we should ask ourselves, "What benefit will my speech bring to me or others?"[181]

  In meetings, there is a tendency by some people to just talk, talk, talk, to hear the sound of their own voice. The people who are considered the wisest and most looked up to in the company often say very little. When they say something it is on point and advances the conversation forward. One of my students took on this challenge of considering the effect of her words before she spoke in meetings, and she found that it made her more effective.

- **Speak out if you are in the habit of keeping your thoughts to yourself.** If you are an introvert, this may seem really hard. Mussar is about moving beyond your comfort zone. You don't need to give the Gettysburg Address. Ask a question in a meeting. If that is too big a step, ask your question after the meeting.

- **Say only positive things about other people.** Withholding praise is harmful if only because we have lost an opportunity to uplift someone else. Look for ways that you can genuinely show praise or appreciation for people. Really look at someone and connect with them, and try to find a way to praise something about them to their face.

- **Do not participate in gossip.** Rabbi Telushkin teaches that when we gossip, we lose an opportunity to genuinely connect with the person we are speaking with.[182] You don't need to lec-

---

181 Levin, *Cheshbon HaNefesh*, 165.
182 Telushkin, 5.

ture the other person or self-righteously declare that you are now above gossip. One way to gently implement this practice is not to respond or give positive feedback to the gossip. Most people will quickly stop. If not, say you need to go and don't have time to listen. Alternatively, ask a question that will help you get to know the other person better.

- **Create a time of silence.** Whether you speak out or not, I enjoin you to try creating a time of silence. This may mean morning meditation, or perhaps no music or news in the car. We can only hear God in times of silence. If we have thoughts, music, or stimulation from the outside blaring in our heads, we will miss subtle cues and connections to God and the world around us.

- **Meditate longer.** While you are practicing silence, increase the time of your meditation. Instead of meditating three minutes, meditate for five minutes. If your norm is five minutes, then raise that number to fifteen minutes. See how long you can bring silence into your life.

- **Don't yell or speak harshly.** The Bible says, "The words of the wise, spoken softly, are accepted," and the Talmud teaches that "one should always speak softly to people."[183] Both verses are teaching an important lesson: if you yell or speak harshly, people will not hear your message. Find a way to soften the way you speak to others.

---

183 Koheles 9:17 and Yoma 86a.

Better to surf the waves of life than get pounded or swept away.

Chapter Fifteen

◆

Equanimity

I teach equanimity later than many other Mussar instructors because it is easy to talk about but hard to practice. As one of my former students once said, "I'm a good test taker. I know how to give the right answer in class. I'm not so good in the real world."

When I first started studying Mussar, I wanted to jump to equanimity right away, which is what I felt I really needed. The Hebrew word for equanimity literally translates as "calmness of the soul." I tend to swing from being super excited to super disappointed. The big highs and lows are tiring. To be honest, in my mind equanimity really meant getting rid of the downs while keeping the elation and excitement. Unfortunately, it doesn't work that way.

Assumption: We All Have Free Will But It Is Not Always Accessible

A short mental exercise: try not to think of chocolate right now. Whatever you do, don't think about chocolate—certainly not about dark chocolate.

How did that go?

Chapter 15

While we have free will over some things, free will gets shaky when it comes to controlling our own thoughts or emotions. Have you ever felt "taken over" by a thought or a distraction? Something happens, and it gnaws at you like a dog that won't let go of a splintered bone. The more we try not to think about it, the worse it becomes. When we are distracted by our thoughts—either upset or elated—there is a significant impact on our actions. For example, we are prone to absent-minded lapses such as putting the television remote in the freezer. Here again, it is hard for me to connect free will to mistaking my remote for a frozen treat.

The more significant the emotional disruption, the less access we have to our free will; thus, there is a more drastic impact on our behavior. For example, as we saw in the last chapter, an angry person will say things that they would never say when calm—things that can damage a relationship forever. Rabbi Levin, one of the nineteenth-century Mussar masters, describes this loss of control in terms of the battle between the evil inclination and the good inclination. Rabbi Levin wrote that when a man's mind is settled, "man has free choice to force his thoughts on exercising his sovereignty [over his animal spirit], and to devise strategies that activate or restrain the animal spirit."[184] (Levin called the evil inclination the animal spirit.) In contrast, Levin continues,

> When his mind is agitated, a fearful darkness falls upon him and his council and strength are taken from him…Or a perverse animal spirit grabs hold of him, dragging him over thorns and briers.[185]

As one who is prone to getting carried away, I can relate to the metaphor of being dragged over thorns and briars. I have a vivid memory of standing in the office of the head of the algorithm group and screaming that resources needed to be diverted from one project onto my "higher priority project" because of an unexpected setback. Two things made this episode particularly shameful:

---

184 Levin, *Cheshbon HaNefesh*, 109.
185 Ibid., 111.

- He would have moved the resources without question and without all the drama.

- The resources were coming from a project managed by my best friend at work, who saw my entire outburst. She, too, agreed that the resources should move to cover the emergency. However, she felt that the hotheaded and selfish way I approached the situation was a betrayal of our relationship. I spent what felt like hours apologizing, and in a very heartfelt way I felt terrible about my behavior.

There is no question that my buttons were pushed and I "lost it." I was so upset that, for all intents and purposes, I did not really have free will at that moment, yet I am not absolved of the responsibility for the consequences of my actions.

What Is Equanimity?

Mussar teaches that equanimity is the soul trait that governs whether you keep your cool or lose your head. One can lose equanimity because of bad things or when really good things happen. The Hebrew word for this soul trait literally translates as "calmness of the soul." In his book *Accounting of the Soul*, Rabbi Levin wrote, "Rise above events that are inconsequential—both bad and good—for they are not worth disturbing your equanimity."[186]

For many years it was easier for me to understand equanimity by avoiding certain situations or behaviors. For example, I might tell myself not to lose my head and behave as I did in the situation I described above. We all have things that will push our buttons, and my first solution to find equanimity was simply to avoid those situations. As you'll see later in the chapter, this is insufficient at best.

I now think of equanimity as presence, i.e., the ability to stay in the present moment and not let your emotions get the better of you.

---

186 Ibid., 109.

Author Eckhart Tolle has a masterful description of equanimity in his book *The Power of Now*. He correctly points out we have a level of consciousness that sits above the thinking mind. Many people mistakenly equate their thoughts with who they are and consider themselves helpless while streams of thoughts roll through their heads. Tolle describes a "watcher" who can observe the thinking mind. He writes,

> The moment you start watching the thinker, a higher level of consciousness becomes activated. You then begin to realize that there is a vast realm of intelligence beyond thought, that thought is only a tiny aspect of that intelligence.[187]

Equanimity is separating the higher mind from the thinking mind, stepping into the role of watcher. Tolle's concept of a "deeper self—behind or underneath the thought"[188] is who we strive to be when we practice equanimity.

Notice that in equanimity you are not removed from life. As an active participant in the world, you will experience both positive and negative situations. However, you will experience them in a more mindful and less reactive way from this higher level of consciousness.

In addition, equanimity is not the same thing as tranquility. We could lock ourselves away from the world and live a tranquil life without anything to either excite us or upset us. Rabbi Yisroel Salanter wrote, "As long as one lives a life of calmness and tranquility in the service of God, it is clear that he is remote from true service."[189]

What??? This phrase was like a lightning bolt that left me stunned when I first read it. In fact, since leaving the corporate world, I had made it a virtue for myself to avoid stressful situations. For the first two months I did little but play games on Facebook. While this may be understandable given the years of high stress I endured, I clearly was missing the mark spiritually. Rabbi Salanter is teaching that a servant of God is expected to be a part of the world as an active and positive force. If you are unsure about Divinity, you may substitute "humanity"

---

187 Tolle, *The Power of Now*, 16–17.
188 Ibid.
189 Morinis, *Everyday Holiness*, 99.

or "the universe" for God if you prefer. Whatever word you use, we are not here to spend our life avoiding stressful situations. Rather, we are here to find a way to remain engaged without letting the situations stress us out.

When I first began to appreciate that this was what equanimity is all about, I thought to myself, "Easier said than done. How am I supposed to just rise above it, as Rabbi Levin suggested?" I was discouraged and confused. For you, of course, equanimity may come as second nature. We each have our unique spiritual curriculum. This one happened to be harder for me. As you'll see later in my journal entries, it wasn't easy, but I made progress over the course of the two weeks that I share and in subsequent years. Now we'll explore equanimity more deeply, with an eye toward helping you develop your own action plan.

The Spectrum of Equanimity

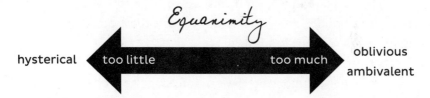

What happens if we have too much equanimity? The concern is that we may become oblivious or ambivalent. If we get to a place where nothing can move us, then we are missing out on the world around us. What kind of a life would we have if we never felt joy or passion? The land where everything is "whatever" is not attractive. On the flip side, with too little equanimity we can become hysterical and feel that we are always on a roller coaster, super excited or feeling really down. These wild swings in mood are unhealthy, exhausting, and make it difficult to bring focus.

The Dalai Lama argues for balanced equanimity as well. Unsurprisingly, he points out that someone in a state of agitation has little bandwidth to notice other people and that anxiety makes it hard to concentrate. I was amazed, however, to read that he said too much calmness can "make us indifferent, like a vegetable." He clarified this statement by explaining that we do not want to withdraw from the world in a "self-satisfied cocoon" but rather remain engaged with the world in a compassionate way.[190]

Equanimity vs. Complacency

Earlier in the chapter I shared Rabbi Salanter's view that tranquility is not the goal of Mussar practice. Judaism is not a religion that has people withdraw from the world to contemplate life. We are expected to engage with the task of repairing the world. There is too much work to be done for us to sit back in our corner. Problems are upsetting, and if we are too tranquil, we are not paying attention to problems sufficiently.

This is not always easy. There are people who will try to keep things in the same place. Some problems are so huge that they may seem intractable or hopeless. The only way to solve those problems is to get in there and get your hands dirty.

There are times when we make progress, and it is natural to sit back and enjoy the moment. If we start feeling like everything is going great and there are no issues whatsoever, perhaps we are becoming complacent. At times complacency has affected my Mussar practice. It begins when things are going well—I am journaling, and I am feeling clear-headed and connected spiritually. Then I will go on vacation. I let the journaling slip and I don't look at my morning mantra quite as often. All of a sudden it has been a month without my Mussar practice: suddenly, something happens and I have lost my cool. It may be something stressful but minor, like a weekend event that wasn't on the family calendar. I know that I would have been able to handle it previously, and now it has become much harder because I have not kept up with my practice. The reason to practice Mussar when things are

---

190 Goleman, *A Force for Good*, 37–38.

going well is to keep our spiritual muscles strong against the day when something challenges us.

Radical Acceptance

The Talmud teaches that how much we earn each year is in the hands of God, and how hard we work does not really affect our earning power.[191] As a recovering workaholic, I immediately dismissed this teaching. If you are unsure about Divinity, I imagine that you are ready to slam this book shut right now, never to pick it up again. Yet the more I thought about it, the more I saw merit to the position. The year I cut my hours from ninety to sixty a week without changing jobs, my pay did not change. Someone who goes to college will earn more money on average, but is computer programming actually harder than a day of manual labor? It is not the level of effort but the type of work that differs.

Consider this situation: two people work equally hard at two different start-up companies. One becomes a millionaire when his company is bought, and the other walks away without even a severance package when his employer goes bust. Whether you are among the minority who think it was God's plan at work or blind luck because both people were working equally hard, the level of individual effort had nothing to do with the sale of the company. In this case (and in many real-life situations), the amount of effort does not, in fact, affect earning power.

In contrast, Judaism teaches that "success or failure at *spiritual pursuits* is completely dependent on man himself, and the degree of success is proportional to the effort expended." Emphasis is mine.[192] If we are faithful to our Mussar practice and work consistently to build our inner world, we will see results.

In order to foster equanimity, we must radically accept what is. Whether your company goes under or makes you a millionaire, you must accept what happens from the standpoint of the watcher

---

191 *Pirkei Avos Treasury*, 42.
192 Ibid.

described earlier. This does not mean that you can't feel sad or happy, and it certainly doesn't mean that you remain passive, cynical, or disengaged. It means that you internally accept what is and decide how and whether to respond from a place of balance and calm.

Rabbi Chaim Vital (1543–1620) required his students to have achieved equanimity before he would take them as a disciple. He explained that they should feel neither pleasure when honored by another nor pain when insulted. He told one student who was not bothered by insults but felt pleasure from compliments that he was not ready to be his disciple. He said, "Go and surrender your heart even more, a true surrendering, until your heart has attained equanimity."[193]

Surrender is a key concept in Tolle's book *The Power of Now*. According to Tolle, surrender is "yielding to rather than opposing the flow of life." Tolle focuses on surrender in situations when things are not going well. When we fight what is, we feel pain. When we surrender, we become empowered to objectively respond to the situation.[194]

The Right Amount of Worry

The medieval Mussar classic *The Ways of the Tzaddikim (Orchot Tzaddikim)* includes a chapter called "The Gate of Worry" that explores the role of worry in a good life.[195] Many of us think of worry as a negative, and rightly so. Indeed, the text says, "Worry and sorrow erode the heart and are the sickness of the body."[196] Today we know this is literally true: stress degrades the immune system[197] and increases our susceptibility to a host of diseases, including diabetes, heart disease, and reflux.[198]

Once I shared a car ride with a friend who was worried about an upcoming event she had helped plan. She didn't like the flyer and

193 Morinis, *Every Day, Holy Day*, 226.
194 Tolle, *The Power of Now*, 205.
195 Zaloshinsky, *The Ways of the Tzaddikim*, 219–28.
196 Ibid., 219.
197 American Psychological Association, "Stress Weakens the Immune System."
198 Angvall, "Stress! Don't Let It Make You Sick."

thought she should have asked the speaker to focus on a different topic. The more she talked, rehashing the conversations and email exchanges she had had with various people, the more agitated she became. The more agitated she became, the more agitated I became. Finally, I blurted out, "This is out of your control and is in God's hands." She wasn't happy with the comment at the time, but when the event was about to start, the room was packed with people. We made eye contact from across the room, and we both smiled.

Many of you may not believe that attendance at the event was in any way mediated by God's plan. That is okay. I hope, however, that you can interpret my comments on a metaphorical level. At a certain point, we need to release the outcome of our choices to the universe and accept the result from a place of equanimity.

You might find this idea of "just release the outcome" confusing. Here again, Tolle's framework from *The Power of Now* is helpful. Tolle explains that when you worry about the future, you are simply rehearsing what could happen based on conditioning of the mind by "all of your past history as well as the collective cultural mindset you have inherited."[199] Confusion is a function of what Tolle calls the thinking mind (or what we call the evil inclination) trying to assert itself. Letting go is not logical. When it comes to the future, logic is impossible because we cannot predict the future. All we can do is make guesses based on past experience and our own cultural biases, which brings us back to Tolle's point above. So, if you find yourself confused, smile because it means that you are making progress. Watch the confusion and continue letting go. Practice enthusiasm and trust. Just let the outcome go.

Sometimes worry can be a habit. We start to question our decisions even though we have no new information. One of the best practices in business is not to revisit a decision unless there is new information. In a similar way, we can train ourselves not to fret over decisions that we've made. Maybe they were the right decisions, maybe they were the

---

199 Tolle, *The Power of Now*, 18.

wrong decisions, but the reality is that most decisions are not all that important.

Please stop for a moment and think about this statement: *Most decisions are not important.* How did you react? There was a time when I would have dismissed it out of hand. Excess self-importance is a humility issue that we first explored in chapter 5. The more we can let go of our self-importance, the less we will worry and the more equanimity we will have.

Dial Back Your Excitement

In the beginning of the chapter I shared that I tend to swing high and low in my life, and I have wanted to keep the happy and get rid of the sad. Unfortunately, things do not work that way. However, I have found that if I limit my excitement, it actually helps remove some of the lows.

For example, in the fall of 2012 my favorite baseball team, the San Francisco Giants, was on the verge of winning its second World Series in three years. In the bottom of the ninth inning there were two outs and Miguel Cabrera, the best hitter in the American league, was at bat for Detroit, representing the winning run.

The count went to two strikes, and Cabrera fouled off pitch after pitch. My brain started racing: *One more strike and the Giants are going to win…wow, that will be their second World Series…there will be another parade!* I found myself getting more and more excited. Then I started to get anxious: *If they lose today, they could go on and lose the whole World Series.*

At the time I was practicing equanimity. Out of the blue, I realized that the more my mind was racing off into the possible future, the less I was paying attention to the game. I made a conscious effort not to go down that road of becoming super excited. I took a deep breath and was able to be calm and remain in the moment.

When Sergio Romo, the Giant's relief pitcher, threw a fastball instead of a slider and struck out Cabrera, I was still super happy and excited. However, I did not have an overlay of super franticness. I was much calmer, and I remember the moment with a richness that I might not have if I had allowed my adrenaline free rein. In the following month I noticed that things that normally would have brought me down didn't have the effect on me that I anticipated they would. By limiting my reactions to positive experiences, I strengthened my soul and made it resilient to the downs that came later.

Daily Practice

Mantra

"Better to surf the waves of life than get pounded or swept away."

In his book *Everyday Holiness,* Alan Morinis uses a great analogy for equanimity: life is like ocean waves breaking upon the shore.[200] Sometimes a big wave will come along that can carry us out to sea or pound us into the sand. Equanimity teaches us to surf the waves and prevents us from getting swept out to sea or being crushed by waves. The waves of life will always be there; with practice and training we will have the spiritual tools to navigate.

Observe

We all have things that push our buttons. For all that I've talked about my ups and downs, there are some things that are easy for me (e.g., public speaking) that cause many other people to fret with fear and worry. Strengthening equanimity is about decreasing the number of situations that cause us to lose our equilibrium and reducing the intensity of the disruption.

Your first step in strengthening your equanimity is to understand how your equanimity is activated. As you go through the day, pay attention to the circumstances that push your buttons. Loss of equanimity can happen in many ways that do not involve acting out. You may become distracted by incessant thoughts or worries. As much as possible, try to be granular. For example, "work stress" is a very wide category and will not tell you much about your spiritual curriculum. In contrast, if you notice that you become upset about the timing and

---

200 Morinis, *Everyday Holiness,* 100.

scope of work assignments, the underlying issue may be order. Alternatively, if sarcastic comments make you lose your confidence, the underlying issue is humility.

Record your observations in your journal.

From My Journal

I noticed an interesting progression in my journal entries over the first two weeks I practiced equanimity. Here are three selections:

Third Day: Noticed that my equanimity is thrown off when my phone calls or email messages are not returned. I did okay today with the dentist not calling me back.

Fifth Day: Really struggling with this soul trait. Trying to talk myself out of the need to do this practice, but equanimity is clearly an issue for me because I become so upset over things like not having my phone calls returned. I feel mentally tired like I am working on Mussar all the time.

Tenth Day: Failure of humility—was criticized on LinkedIn by someone I know that threw me. Spent too many cycles thinking how to respond—I didn't need to respond at all. Lost equanimity, spent time I didn't have on the stupid poll. More importantly, I should have been more humble, not acted like I had something to prove.

Very good discussion today with my study partner about this. Equanimity comes from being centered—a oneness with everything and everyone. If I had recognized the Divine in the person who made the comment and in myself, what does it matter what he thinks about this issue? What another person thinks about me is none of my business and is outside my control. Both humility and honor are in play.

Act

Rabbi Simcha Zissel Ziv said, "A person who has mastered peace of mind has gained everything. To obtain peace of mind, you need to be at peace with your emotions and desires."[201] We can bring equanim-

---

201 Pliskin, "Peace of Mind."

ity toward balance in one of two ways. Some actions, such as meditation and visualization, increase our general resilience to stress. Other actions will be based on the observations you make about the underlying soul traits when your buttons are pushed.

Practice the following visualizations every day to strengthen your equanimity muscles:

- **Visualization 1.** Sit in a comfortable place and close your eyes. Start to think about something that causes you to feel anxious. Just gently bring it up in your mind until you start to feel that stress in your stomach. Hold your hands on either side of your stomach and visualize holding that anxiety between your hands. You are the watcher. Watching the emotions will create a space and allow you to experience a higher level of consciousness. See the emotions, and then experience yourself watching the emotions. You are in control, and your internal true self cannot be touched by the outside world. When you start to feel stress during the day, become the watcher.

- **Visualization 2.** Close your eyes, and visualize yourself driving along the highway. Gently think of something that causes you stress, and place it in the car in front of you. The car wants to go faster, but you mentally pull the car back. You are in control of the car and pull it all the way back, to the right of your car. Breathe slowly and deeply as you smoothly drive your car. Look over to the car carrying your stress as it bounces along the shoulder. It is filled with screaming teenagers who are trying to drive away, but you are in control. Breathe deeply as you smoothly drive your car and mentally prevent the other car from driving out of control. Be the watcher. Observe the chaos in the other car but know that you are safe and in control in your car.

- **Identify a soul trait imbalance that causes you to lose your equanimity.** After observing and journaling for a few days, identify the things that consistently push your buttons.

They can be big things or small things. In some ways, addressing the small buttons is better because you will make progress more quickly and put yourself on a more solid spiritual foundation. Answer the following questions in your journal:

- What is the underlying soul trait that is in play?

- Write the name of the soul trait here: _____

- What is one small change that you can make to bring this trait toward balance?

Write your intention in your journal. Each night record whether you did or did not act according to your intention. Reflect on the experience as you write. The act of writing and replaying gives you a chance to be the watcher, an impartial reporter describing what happened. No judgment, no consequences, just writing.

Fear consequences but not action.

Chapter Sixteen

◆

Fear of Consequences

Chapters 16 and 17 address two separate but related soul traits: fear of consequences and awe of majesty. In the classic Mussar tradition, these are combined into a single soul trait called *yirah*. Yirah is a Hebrew word that does not translate directly into English. It can be translated as "fear of God" or as "awe of God" and is a fusion of both at the same time. Yirah is one of the most complex, esoteric, and important soul traits. In my view, the fear aspect and the awe aspect are sufficiently different to study separately.

I heard a story once about a master piano teacher who made her students practice each hand separately for months before she allowed them to practice both hands at the same time. When they finally did integrate the two, the results were spectacular. In this book you will only be practicing yirah one-handed. As your practice grows over time, you will put what you have learned together for great effect. This chapter focuses on the "fear of God" aspect of yirah, which I have reframed to the core issue: fear of consequences.

Chapter 16

Assumption: We Are Driven By a Conflict Between Good Inclination and Evil Inclination

Remember that the evil inclination corresponds to those deep emotions and feelings that come from our amygdala. The amygdala is responsible for our fight or flight responses, sexual drives, and emotional responses. I don't think it is an accident that vertebrates evolved sexual urges and fear responses before the more social parts of the brain developed. Without exaggeration, I can say that we would not be here without the amygdala's role in keeping us out of danger and pushing us to propagate. When these base instincts go unchecked, however, we get into trouble.

Fear has been keeping us alive for millions of years, and we are finely tuned to recognize danger, which sets off a physiological cascade of responses. Yet our modern brains cannot tell the difference between a real threat (such as a large predator) and non-lethal stressors (such as aggressive behavior at work).

Fortunately, we are more than just our urges and fears. We also have the good inclination, the impulses that come from the prefrontal cortex, the uniquely human part of the brain that is involved with relationships, higher thinking, and logic. We need both the good and the evil inclinations in order to be a complete person.

The evil inclination has a head start, and both the Jewish tradition and modern science explain why. For example, Judaism teaches that children do not develop the good inclination until they are thirteen.[202] Modern psychology and neurobiology research has shown that the prefrontal cortex, which I associate with the good inclination, continues to develop until humans reach the age of twenty-five.[203] In addition, our brain can react to fear over 100 times faster than our conscious brain's ability to perceive the danger.[204] Given the large head start the

---

202 Bialik and Ravnitsky, eds., *The Book of Legends*, 538:23.
203 National Public Radio, "Brain Maturity Extends Well Beyond Teen Years."
204 "The Amygdala & Emotions," http://www.effective-mind-control.com /amygdala.html.

Fear of Consequences

evil inclination has over the good inclination, is it any surprise that it is a continuous effort to keep it in check?

What Is Fear of Consequences?

Mussar teaches that it is not simply enough to learn the Torah; one must act on it too. As it says in the Talmud, "One who has the Torah but not fear of heaven is like a treasurer who has been given the inner keys but not the outer keys. Through which door can he enter?"[205] To us a more modern analogy, having the Torah without fear of heaven is like having car keys without a key to unlock the garage; it won't get you where you need to go. The sage Rava is even more explicit, explaining that if one exclusively labors to study the Torah but not fulfill its laws, one will inherit punishment in the next world and miss out on the great joys of life in this one.[206]

Traditional Mussar teaches that fear of God and fear of heaven are key to developing good behavior. This is based on the assumption that God knows everything we do, and we will face the music in the next world if we do not conduct ourselves properly in this world. I personally am not a fan of this view of Divinity, and for those who are skeptical about God, I suspect the fire-and-brimstone reputation of the God of the Old Testament is part of the reason. For example, the daily Shema prayer says that if you listen and follow the commandments, there will be rain and a good life. If you do not follow the commandments, "anger of the Lord will blaze against you, and He will close the heavens and there will not be rain, and the earth will not give you its fullness, and you will perish quickly from the good land the Lord gives you."[207]

If we step back from a literal reading and leave behind the concept that God is rewarding and punishing us according to how we act, there is an underlying lesson: actions have consequences. I have no doubt that if you live a life making your best efforts to live up to

205 Talmud Shabbos 31a-b; Zaloshinsky, *The Ways of the Tzaddikim*, 609.
206 Zaloshinsky, *The Ways of the Tzaddikim*, 609.
207 Deuteronomy 11:17.

Jewish values, you will have a better life than if you ignore them. Each day we are faced with choice points, where we have an opportunity to take the path of least resistance or the higher road. In fact, Rabbi Ira Stone explains that fear of God refers to the fear of "the responsibilities that are always with us, and the consequences of not meeting those responsibilities."[208]

Fear of God or Fear of Consequences?

For some people the injunction to fear God brings forth the fire-and-brimstone images of God that are often associated with the Old Testament. In my opinion, and as Alan Morinis wrote in his book, this is a tough sell.[209] Fear can only go so far. "You better be good or else!" has not been a good strategy the times I have tried it as a parent; I do not think it works well with adults either.

At the same time, we do need to have a healthy respect for consequences. The book of Proverbs says, "Fear of the Lord is the beginning of wisdom."[210] I certainly see that point, which is also explained in Proverbs: "The prudent person sees trouble ahead and hides, but the naive continue on and suffer the consequences."[211] We can't really know what will happen in the future, but we need to appreciate that what we say and what we do will change the world. I see the fear of consequences as the embodiment of the phrase "God only knows what will happen if…" Wisdom is being able to appreciate what we don't know and realizing that when we open the door, we can never be sure what will come in or what will get out.

Do we need to have God as part of the picture? We can look at consequences in a logical way, and on an intellectual level I totally get it. Wisdom, however, has a spiritual as well as an intellectual component. Wisdom takes into account empathy, feeling, caring for people. In that

---

208 Stone, chapter 5, 1050.
209 Morinis, *Everyday Holiness*, 234.
210 Proverbs 9:10; 111:10, New International Version.
211 Proverbs 22:3, International Standard Version.

sense, Mussar teaches us that the fear of consequences is inseparable from the rest of the practice.

That being said, the soul traits of fear and awe are challenging. I struggle with them, as do many of my students. That is okay. It is worth the effort. Imagine that God appeared to you in the room. The Torah teaches that no one can look upon God and live. Even Moses just caught a glimpse as God passed by and was forever shaken. The Divine Presence is overwhelming. So if God arrived in God's true form, what would you do? Scream? Cry? Crap in your pants from fear? Or would you bow down in an instant, trembling with joy?

These may not be thoughts that many of you ponder in the modern Jewish community, yet put yourself in those shoes for a moment. Allow yourself to feel the fear that you may have done something wrong.

The Spectrum of Fear of Consequences

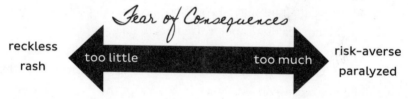

What happens if we have too much fear of consequences? We become risk-averse. We do not move outside of our comfort zone, and in more extreme cases we may not even leave the house. There is no growth in the comfort zone and no comfort in the growth zone.

To grow, we need to leave our comfort zone; there is no other way. Getting ahead in business or doing something extraordinary will require you to learn new skills that you may not want to learn. Several women in my class observed that giving birth requires going beyond your comfort zone both literally and metaphorically.

It is normal to be filled with fears about what lies ahead. In the case of becoming a parent, you ask yourself questions, such as, "What will it be like to have a child? What will happen to my career? Will I ever see my friends again? Will I ever have time for my spouse again?"

These fears could prevent us from moving ahead and having a family. It is incumbent on us to not allow these fears to drive our decisions because fear cannot account for the growth and learning process.

If we have too little fear of consequences, we can become capricious, reckless, or brash. We will go along doing whatever, not worrying about the effect our actions have on ourselves or other people. For example, when we practiced silence we learned that the measure for proper speech is not our intention but the effect our words have on other people. We should have a healthy fear that our words could hurt another.

The Fear Pivot to Overcome Fear of Missing Out

One of the fears that sometimes holds us back is the fear of failure. We might get so worried that we will not be successful that we do not start. To counter the fear of failure, we need to practice a *fear pivot*. Instead of being afraid that you will not be successful, become afraid that you are not making enough attempts to do good.

The Mussar classic *The Ways of the Tzaddikim* devotes an entire chapter to "The Gate of Worry," which discusses the circumstance when we should be more worried, which is "worry for the sake of heaven."[212] The chapter reads as a reminder of how we should worry that we are not practicing Mussar well enough:

> [One] wise in Torah must worry that his deeds are not commensurate with his wisdom; and if he is not, he must worry about not having the ability to probe [his spiritual curriculum]. If he is honored, he must be heedful not to rejoice in that Honor. If he is wise and yet despised in the eyes of the world, he should…worry that being despised will prevent people from accepting his [advice].[213]

I see this as a corollary to the phenomenon of the fear of missing out. On the National Day of Unplugging, which takes place every year

212 Zaloshinsky, *The Ways of the Tzaddikim*, 223.

213 Ibid., 225–27. The brackets indicate places where I have substituted more modern language. The original text reads "probe *the roots of saintliness*" and "prevent people from accepting his *rebuke*."

on a Sabbath in March, people turn off all of their electronic devices. On that day I turned off social media and my cell phone but I continued to watch television. I invited my Twitter followers to participate with me and then asked people to tweet about their experiences. One person stated that it was really hard, and all day she had a lot of fear of missing out.

I wondered what it was that she was afraid of missing. If we are always afraid that we are missing out, then we spend our time checking email and social media constantly. As a consequence, we lose touch with the day-to-day world around us. We lose opportunities to connect with the people who might be in the same room, the same town, or the same coffee shop that we are in.

We can mindfully transform the fear of missing out into the fear of not making connections with people around us. If we spend all of our time and energy trying to keep up with everything that is happening in social media, we have a certainty that we will become stressed and disconnected from the people around us. We certainly will not be able to be fully present.

Fear Means Something Else Is Out of Balance

As we learned in chapter 10, when we are feeling the desire to be untruthful, it is because another trait is out of balance. In a similar way, if we are feeling fear, it is because something else is out of balance. For example, if we are afraid that we'll miss something, maybe it is because our humility is out of balance. Bringing humility back into balance can restore our confidence and lessen the fear. If we are afraid that we may lose something, perhaps order is out of balance. Instead of obsessively putting things away to combat the fear, work on becoming less controlling by trusting in the universe.

The soul traits are all interconnected—after all, each is but a part of the soul, a means to bring about change without becoming overwhelmed by the soul's complexity. Fear is such a primal emotion that we cannot ignore it, and at the same time we cannot let it dominate our lives.

Chapter 16

Daily Practice

Mantra

"Fear consequences but not action." Or, if you wish the more traditional view: "The fear of God is the beginning of wisdom.[214] Fear of consequences is the beginning of wisdom."

As I wrote earlier in the chapter, fear of God is a tough one. It brings to mind the image of an angry father yelling, "I'll put the fear of God into you," which is an antiquated model of parenting. If we step back from our twenty-first-century sensibilities and think about the root idea, something interesting happens. This angry father figure was, in a clumsy way, trying to teach a lesson about consequences: if you do something wrong, something bad will happen. If you do something morally wrong, your punishment may be for eternity. This is not the lesson that American Mussar teaches, although it is pervasive in certain parts of the medieval Mussar literature.

There is another parenting example that comes to mind. It is the look on a child's face when the parent says, "I'm disappointed in you because I know you are better than this." In many ways, this is the modern equivalent of "I'll put the fear of God into you." Now the punishment is a disappointed parent as opposed to violence or pain. In both cases, the goal is to learn how to anticipate the consequences of your actions and thus prevent unnecessary pain.

Of the different mantra options above, I prefer "fear consequences but not action" because so often fear leads to paralysis. If you find yourself stuck because you are afraid, it is time to look for ways of taking action. For example, many people don't look for a new job because they are afraid that no one will hire them. Instead, they remain in an unhappy and unhealthy work environment. By shifting the focus of the fear to consequences, you now have to think about the consequences of inaction, and the primal fear that "no one will want me" opens the door to additional Mussar work. Which soul trait might lead you to feel unworthy or inadequate?

---

214 Proverbs 9:10.

Dealing with a negative work environment is not easy, and the decision to look for a new job should not be taken lightly. What this practice and mantra will help you do is approach it from a place of wisdom—thoughtful contemplation—instead of fear.

Observe

As you go through your day, observe when you become afraid. Is it the raw fear of panic or is it a fear from too much analysis? Do you become paralyzed or find yourself reluctant to take action?

Conversely, be on the lookout for times when you are behaving in a rash or reckless way, which is an indicator that you are not sufficiently considering the consequences of your actions. These habits may be so ingrained that you do not notice how they are affecting your behavior. You may also want to ask people close to you—friends, family, or even coworkers—if they see you as risk-averse or as a risk taker.

Become the watcher. Without self-judgment, observe as much as you can about the circumstances where your fear of consequences is out of balance. Write the details in your journal. The more you learn, the better you'll be able to understand the underlying soul traits causing the fear, which will empower thoughtful correction.

From My Journal

Glad I found a way to put the family first. My younger daughter is feeling much better tonight. I didn't work during the day when she was home sick because of fear of wrongdoing. I wanted to be there for her because I was afraid of not doing my parental job.

Act

Fear is an advanced soul trait. As you are now familiar with practicing many other soul traits, look for other soul traits to help bring fear into balance, such as the following:

- **Trust can overcome fear and worry.** If you are a worrier, select one thing that you worry about on a regular basis. Wear a rubber band to remind you that the outcome is in the hands of the universe.

- **Enthusiasm.** Having too little fear is similar to having too much enthusiasm, in that both result in rash or thoughtless behavior. A more thoughtful approach to action is called for, which can be achieved with a greater appreciation of the consequences of your actions. Each day list three things in your journal that you did, and write down all of the consequences of your actions. While honor and silence focus on the consequences for others of your actions, here you should focus on the consequences for yourself.

  For example, a thoughtless comment could hurt someone else's feelings, which is itself a bad thing. What further damage can this do to you? For example, a friend once told me of an email exchange where someone in another department tried to take credit for something he did. Although he was mad, he chose to reply privately and not shame the other person. One year later this person became his manager, and soon was a staunch supporter and ally. My friend was quite deliberate in that he did not want to make an enemy because "you never know."

- **Equanimity can help you combat fear and worry.** When you begin to worry, take a deep breath and step into equanimity, watching the worry from a place of calm.

I play a small part in something greater than myself.

Chapter Seventeen
◆
Awe of Majesty

The first year I attended the Mussar Institute's Kallah (retreat), one of the faculty began her session by sharing her first experience with Mussar. After a rabbi explained trust to her, she told him that sounded too hard. In response, he told her to study yirah, the Hebrew word that fuses both awe and fear. The audience laughed because we all understood how incredibly difficult yirah is. As I explained in the last chapter, I have chosen to teach yirah as its separate components. Awe is the more difficult of the two, which means that you have more potential upside when you practice it. Rabbis have been known to weep in frustration trying to access yirah. Yirah can seem mystical and esoteric, which is not what we expect from the everyday spirituality we've come to love about Mussar, yet we are not free to ignore awe.

Wouldn't it be cool to infuse everyday living with a sense of wonder and mystery? If you are a parent, you've seen your children marvel at ordinary things like automatic doors or sprinklers that send water shooting up at regular intervals around your lawn. I invite you to keep an open mind to learning the art of experiencing wonder every day. Wonder is a battery that never runs out of power. When you learn to tap into it, you'll never run out of spiritual energy.

Chapter 17

Assumption: We All Carry a Divine Spark That Is Occluded By Our Baggage

The divine spark is particularly prevalent in people, but of course the Divine is everywhere. There is so much wonder in the world. If you believe that God created the universe or that there is something higher and greater out there, you can find evidence all around you once you know how to look for it.

Go to a national park and see the beauty of the mountains and the forests, the majesty of waves crashing against cliffs, and the perfection in the spiral of a seashell. Our lungs can pull life-giving oxygen out of the very air. The Baal Shem Tov said, "The world is full of wonders and miracles, but we take our little hand and we cover our eyes and see nothing."[215]

What Is the Awe of Majesty?

Awe is defined as referential respect with an element of dread or wonder. As I explained in chapter 16, the awe of majesty is one of two English translations of the Hebrew word yirah, the other being fear. Awe is about appreciating your place in the endless possibility of the universe; as it says in the Talmud, "Know before Whom you stand."[216] These words are written in Hebrew in many synagogues above the ark as a reminder to maintain a sense of decorum during services. The great twentieth-century philosopher and rabbi Abraham Joshua Heschel taught that we can and should cultivate the awareness of the Divine everywhere we go.[217] Whether you believe in the Divine or the universal, we all have the opportunity to experience awe—the overwhelming feeling of something greater, something amazing beyond words.

Rabbi Amy Eilberg described how the birth of her daughter, Penina, helped her reconnect to awe in the world. Eilberg wrote that as Penina

---

215 http://www.livinglifefully.com/wonder.htm.
216 B'rachot 28b.
217 Apple, "Know Before Whom You Stand."

experienced joy and wonder at discovering new things, she rediscovered her own ability to "rejoice and exclaim over life's everyday discoveries."[218] Moreover, Rabbi Eilberg found that her entire perception of God was changed from a giver of law to a giver of life. Now she could feel "sanctity in nursing and diaper changing and rocking and comforting."[219] If you are unsure of Divinity, know that awe can help you find the sacred in everyday life.

In addition, awe can inspire us. For example, awe of Michael Phelps, winner of a record eight gold medals in a single Olympics, inspires swimmers. Awe of Bach inspires musicians. Awe of Einstein inspires scientists. Awe of majesty can inspire us to become great people. We can hold the Creator in awe, who gave Phelps, Bach, and Einstein their genius. If you are unsure of Divinity, you can feel awe of the universe for its ability to create such genius. We too have the capacity for greatness—greatness at being ourselves.

Before his death, Rabbi Zusya said, "In the coming world, they will not ask me: 'Why were you not Moses?' They will ask me: 'Why were you not Zusya?'"[220]

Cultivating awe is a counterweight to the natural tendency to get a swelled head and overestimate one's importance in the grand scheme of things. We are all stars in our respective life stories, and who wants to see themselves as a flea on the back of time? A star, by its nature, has a big role. Awe reminds us that our role is actually very small, no matter who we are. There are more than six billion people on this planet, which itself has a complex climate and ecology. We play a very, very, very small part in the cycle of the planet and an infinitely small role in the universe.

Robert Herjavec, multi-millionaire star of the TV series *Shark Tank*, was forced to realize the limitations of human power when his mother was diagnosed with terminal cancer. At first he thought that his wealth

---

218 Umansky, *Four Centuries of Jewish Women's Spirituality*, 283. The article is "The Gifts of First Fruits" (1988) by Amy Eilberg.

219 Ibid., 284.

220 Buber, *Tales of the Hasidim*, 251.

and willpower could turn things around, but he quickly learned that we are powerless against cancer. He wrote, "Cancer doesn't care if you're tall, short, small, large, someone's brother, sister, father or someone's mom. Seemingly without rhyme or reason it strikes, hurting those we love and cutting lives short."[221]

Herjavec learned what it meant to "know before Whom you stand." His awe inspired him to a beautiful dance performance on *Dancing with the Stars* and to share his mother's story to raise awareness of ovarian cancer. Okay, I know it may seem a bit surprising to use a popular show like *Dancing with the Stars* to illustrate awe, but that is exactly my point. It would be a mistake to pigeonhole awe to the big and heavy when it can inspire us to greater heights in the everyday. Suddenly, ordinary day-to-day living becomes a thing of majesty, mystery, and wonder. For example, right now I'm marveling at the great diversity of the fifteen people in line for coffee here at Philz. I see a wide spectrum of age, gender, color, and clothing, all waiting for their chance to pick from among the twenty varieties of coffee beans. Why do they wait ten or more minutes? The coffee is awesome!

The Spectrum of Awe

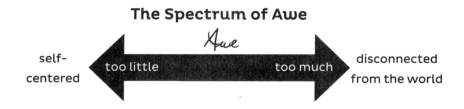

What happens if we have too much awe? We could become disconnected with the world and not take enough action. Sitting around contemplating the universe and marveling at the number of stars without lifting a finger to make the world a better place is not how we are meant to live. Mussar teaches that our primary task is to repair the world, which is enabled by becoming better people. Alternatively, too much awe can lead to rigid thinking that is sometimes in evidence

---

221 Koerner, "'*Dancing with the Stars*' Robert Herjavec."

with followers of Christian, Jewish, or Islamic fundamentalism, who follow teachings that are excessively anchored to one interpretation of the text. Here, people are misappropriating awe. One particularly shameful example occurred a few years ago when Ultra-Orthodox men spit and hurled insults at an eight-year-old girl walking to school because her modest dress did not conform to the exacting standards of this particular Ultra-Orthodox community.[222] This obsession with such exacting and inflexible rules is a dangerous outgrowth of excess awe. A Torah scholar who initiates such unseemly and unethical behavior is reminiscent of men scolded in *Duties of the Heart*, who study Torah only for prestige and do not endeavor to "correct personal faults...neglecting the study of the fundamentals of the religion and the foundations of Torah...[Without practicing the fundamentals] one simply cannot fulfill the commandments."[223] (This is the converse of my favorite saying from the '70s TV show *Kung Fu*: "The body is the arrow, the mind is the bow." In this case, knowing Torah is the bow, but without an arrow to bring its teachings to the world, it is useless.)

Duties of the Heart itself is a source of awe for me. It was written around 1040 in Judeo Arabic, 400 years before the printing press, which means that it was written on a codex of animal skins and was sufficiently copied and preserved such that we can still benefit from its wisdom almost 1,000 years later.[224] I also find it amazing that the descriptions of human behavior are still so spot-on! The inner workings of people have not changed.

If we have too little awe, on the other hand, we become self-centered and cynical. We begin to think that we are the center of the universe and can't see any motivation other than self-interest. We overestimate our own importance, which leads us to treat others badly. Too little awe also can lead to feeling lost in a meaningless universe. Nothing

---

222 Kershner, "Israeli Girl, 8, at Center of Tension over Religious Extremism."

223 ibn Paquda, *Duties of the Heart*, 21.

224 The Bodleian library at Oxford has a copy dating back to 1191, and there is an even older version in Paris. Moritz Steinschneider, *The Hebrew Translations of the Middle Ages and the Jews as Transmitters, Vol. I* (New York and London: Springer, 2013), 75. doi 10.1007/978-94-007-7314-1.

is sacred, nothing matters, which can lead one to question why we should bother living. Awe is one of the things that gives life meaning.

Awe: The Source of Wisdom

According to the Talmud, Rabbi Eliezer said, "Where there is no wisdom, there is no awe. When there is no awe, there is no wisdom."[225] He used the following visual image to explain the point. "One whose deeds are greater than his wisdom, to what is he compared? To a tree with many roots and few branches, whom all the storms in the world cannot budge from its place." Conversely, he said that wisdom without deeds is like a tree with many branches but few roots. One good wind, and over it falls.[226] Rabbi Eliezer went on to quote the book of Jeremiah, which reads, "He shall be as a tree planted upon water, who spreads his roots by the river; who fears not when comes heat, whose leaf is ever lush; who worries not in a year of drought, and ceases not to yield fruit."[227]

Awe, then, allows us to become like the great tree, deeply rooted by the river. When we are filled with awe of majesty, we have an infinite resource to draw upon in times of darkness to help us get through. Yes, we play a small part in this world, but we are a part of this greater whole, and we are never alone. This point is so important I am going to repeat it: *we are a part of this greater whole, and we are never alone.* Rabbi Harold Kushner makes a similar point in this passage from his book *Overcoming Life's Disappointments.* Kushner wrote,

> When Moses says, "Who am I that I should go to Pharaoh?" God answers not by telling Moses who he is, but by telling him who God is, saying, "I will be with you" (Exodus 3:12).[228]

We may feel alienated and cut off, but the source of awe is out there, waiting for us. And we can draw upon awe for strength and wisdom

---

225 *Pirkei Avot* 3:17.

226 Ibid.

227 Ibid., quoting Jeremiah 17:8. See http://www.chabad.org/library/article_cdo/aid/2019/jewish/Chapter-Three.htm for the source of the translation.

228 Kushner, *Overcoming Life's Disappointments*, 20.

when we need it. Even when we don't need it, we can draw upon awe to enrich and energize our lives.

Once when I was driving, I could feel stress taking over. There is no other way to describe it; I was being taken over. As it happened, I could literally feel my peripheral vision constricting. It was like I was looking in a tunnel. My evil inclination was cutting me off from the world. Later that day, I took a walk around the neighborhood to calm down. I slowed down my breathing and reached out to the world. Suddenly, birds were singing. It was like turning on a radio in the middle of your favorite song. There was music when just an instant before there was silence. The music of the birds had been there all along. I only had to open my ears to hear it.

Awe of Majesty: The Keystone Soul Trait

You've now studied twelve soul traits, and I hope you've remembered that a soul trait is just a convenient way to describe the indescribable soul. We've seen how the various traits interact and how some, like humility, trust, and enthusiasm, are particularly central. Awe and its shadow, fear, are the keystones of all the soul traits. The medieval Mussar book *The Ways of the Tzaddikim* describes awe as the knot that holds a string of pearls in place. The knot

> secures all of the good traits, and if you remove it, all of the good traits will depart from you. And if you do not have good traits, you do not have Torah and *mitzvos* [commandments], for all of Torah hinges upon the perfection of one's traits.[229]

In other words, we need to have a sense of wonder, a sense of something greater than ourselves in order to be motivated to become better. We want to become part of something bigger. We want to better ourselves, and awe sets the bar for our best selves.

Remember the soul trait profile that you created way back in chapter 2? Contemplate the circular dashed line at 5.5 on the spider diagram; 5.5 is the point of balance (see figure 9, next page). Mussar teaches

---

229 Zaloshinsky, *The Ways of the Tzaddikim*, 17.

that only the Divine is balanced in all traits. Whether you have a literal belief in the Divine or a more abstract concept like a higher power or the laws of nature, there is an absolute out there to set the bar, a place of perfection we can all strive for. In American Mussar, the circle on the soul trait profile, the point of balance, is the state of perfection we all strive for but can never achieve. How does it make you feel when you read that you can never achieve perfection? What soul trait is in play?

Figure 9: *The Circle Sets the Bar for Balance*

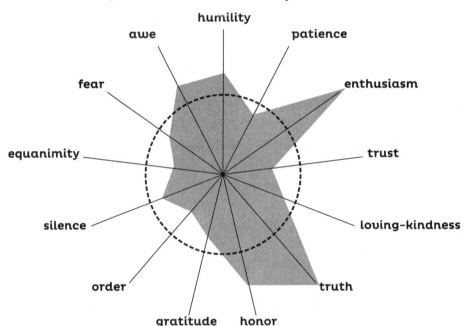

Awe and AA Awe Can Help You Change

Now that you've been practicing Mussar for months, you've learned a lot. I'm sure you've run into some areas where it is really hard to change. For example, maybe patience is a roadblock you just can't get by. As hard as you try, you can't seem to find a choice point—before you know it, you are raging mad despite your best efforts. Awe can help you overcome such momentous obstacles in the soul. As an example, we'll look outside of Mussar practice to twelve-step recovery programs like Alcoholics Anonymous (AA).

Twelve-step programs use spirituality as a means to alter addictive behavior. The AA *Big Book* has sections that read like a Mussar text. For example:

> No one can expect to perfectly adhere to these principles. We are not saints. The point is that we are willing to grow along spiritual lines. The principles that we have set down are guides to progress. We claim spiritual progress rather than spiritual perfection.[230]

AA also teaches its practitioners to progress "one step at a time," which is again very similar to the approach we practice in Mussar. When we are stuck and feel unable to progress, we can take lessons from the AA approach to addiction.

Addiction itself is generally considered outside the scope of regular Mussar practice because an addictive behavior by definition does not really have choice points but falls within the realm of the evil inclination. For example, when a junkie only cares about her next fix, is she really making a choice when she does whatever it takes to get the money? Practitioners of AA recognize that they are powerless over their addiction and surrender to a higher power for assistance. In Mussar terms, they have so lost the power to choose that they need an outside power to give them the strength to change. Turning to a higher power in this way is an act of awe.

While I hope you are not struggling with addiction, many of us have habits so deeply ingrained that our behavior seems closer to addiction than free choice. Awe can help you overcome these stubborn habits. This idea may be uncomfortable for you, and it certainly is not part of the mainstream culture, Jewish or otherwise, in America today.

Yet you may be familiar with a distorted echo of this practice: hero worship. I live in Silicon Valley, a culture built on the legend of Bill Hewlett and Dave Packard, who started the tech giant HP in a garage. We are regaled with tales of Steve Jobs, Elon Musk, and Mark

---

230 *Alcoholics Anonymous: The Big Book*, chapter 5, http://www.aa.org/assets /en_US/en_bigbook_chapt5.pdf.

Zuckerberg, which come with an implicit message that if we model ourselves on the giants of industry, we too can achieve greatness. Rather than model ourselves on flawed human beings within the limited scope of business practice, why not model our behavior on the Divine?

To that end, the book of Deuteronomy says that we should walk in the ways of the Divine,[231] which Mussar refines to specific behaviors. For example, God is patient, so we should be patient. God is kind, so we should be kind. God is merciful, so we should be merciful. God comforts the mourning and heals the sick, so we should comfort the bereaved and care for the ill.[232]

If our block toward balance is not in one of these areas specified, we can keep in mind that circle on the soul trait profile graph—that point of balance that we can all strive for. And awe can help in more general ways: allow yourself to experience greatness. Experience the awesome and you will be changed. It can give you the small nudge you need to progress toward balance.

Are You Stuck Because of Too Much Awe?

Just as awe can help you become unstuck, it is possible that you are stuck because of too much awe. Maybe your boss or the immensity of the task intimidates you. Recently, the fight-or-flight reflex that we were taught as kids has been replaced by the fight, flight, or freeze reflex out of recognition that one reaction to stress is to freeze.

Imagine for a moment that you were in the presence of the Divine. For those of you unsure of Divinity, I invite you to participate in this as a thought exercise. Imagine that God walks into the room, except of course God is in no way human. God is a supreme force, such that even Moses, the greatest of the prophets, threw himself down in fear and awe when in God's presence. How would you react?

Have you ever met someone you were in awe of, whom you admired so greatly that you were unable to speak? Many a romantic comedy

231 Deuteronomy 8:6, 19:9, 26:17.
232 Sotah 14a.

features a scene with the guy/gal babbling incoherently when they first meet the object of their desire because they are "dumbstruck" with love. Speaking to someone we admire and revere is not easy, especially if we feel that they are so much better than us. For example, I used to get nervous and unable to be myself around senior management when I was in the corporate world.

Judaism anticipates this reaction, and before major prayers we say, "Lord, open my lips; then my mouth will praise you."[233] On those rare occasions when I went to services when I was younger, I treated this as a throwaway sentence. After all, my mouth is open when I talk and sing or I am reading in my head. Now that I practice awe, I understand the reason behind the request—if you really think of prayer as direct communication with something greater, it can be really intimidating! If I got nervous talking to the CEO, how much more so would I feel talking to the Creator?

The prayer to "open my lips" is a request to the Divine for help to overcome the discomfort of speaking to one so much greater than we are. Note that the request is only for help with the first step—just help me get my mouth open, just help me get unstuck. Help me overcome my fright and help me get started. With many things in life, the first step is the hardest. Once we start down the ski slope, there is no turning back.

In the Daily Practice section of this chapter, I'll suggest a method to pray for help if you get stuck.

Awesome Tasks Over Awesome Amounts of Time

It is hard to come up with a figure in Jewish history more revered than Moses, the greatest of the prophets. Among other things, Moses led the Israelites out of slavery and delivered the Torah. Yet at the end of his life, Moses never reached the Promised Land. There are many interpretations of this story. Some think that Moses was being punished because he had defied God and because he had killed an Egyptian. But

---

233 Psalms 51:17, *Complete Jewish Bible.*

Rabbi Tarfon provides another interpretation in the Talmud. He said, "It is not incumbent on you to complete the task, but neither are you at liberty to desist from it."[234]

Rabbi Tarfon was teaching that sometimes our life's work may not be completed in our lifetime. Even if Moses had crossed the river, the task would not be complete; there were lands to be won, a king to be anointed, and a temple to be built. Sure, it might feel more just if he got to stand in the land of Canaan, but life doesn't always work out that way.

Time is more infinite than any of us could possibly experience. The universe is bigger than any one of us can touch. To think that we could experience all of time and space is so ludicrous that it hardly makes sense to write about it. We cannot even experience all of what is happening around us at every moment of the day. If a historical figure like Moses eventually has to step away for someone else to complete the work, then we need to accept the same idea for ourselves.

Do we only derive meaning from the completion of a task? I will be honest: I struggle with the concept of "it's about the journey, not the destination." I know my personality; I love to finish things and check the boxes. The destination is important, and I resonate with the destination. There is nothing wrong with a destination—nothing wrong with having a dream or goal as something to set your sights on. But we cannot allow a destination to hold the rest of our life hostage. Our chance of happiness at the destination is no greater than our chance of happiness right now in ordinary life.

We need to realize that there are many steps to reach a goal. Today a kidney transplant is a routine medical procedure in America. How many hundreds of years of research gave us enough knowledge so that we could transplant a kidney? Someone had to discover the kidney by dissecting the human body for the first time. Someone had to figure out what the kidney did. We had to learn about blood types. We had to learn how to do surgery in a reliable way that did not kill the patient. We need to have antibiotics to prevent infection. There were years of

---

234 *Pirkei Avot* 2:16.

small details that needed to be discovered and worked out before we could perform the miracle of kidney transplantation. In fact, we are still learning about the process, and we are still making it better. The people hundreds of years ago making discoveries had no idea that their work was laying the foundation for the miracle of kidney transplantation. Their awe and their curiosity about the universe helped propel them forward.

Let Awe Carry You Out of the Comfort Zone

In the last chapter we learned that too much fear keeps us in our comfort zone. Awe can inspire us to leave the comfort zone. For example, having children requires that we leave our comfort zone. If we are too afraid of the changes kids will bring to our life, the difficulties of childbirth or pregnancy, or the responsibility of providing for a young life, then we may never go ahead and have children. On the other hand, we could focus on the awe of bringing a new life into the world and of having a family, continuing our genetic line and the family name. All of these bigger things can inspire us to move ahead and have a family.

We can also use awe to inspire success. When I was a scientist studying the intricacies of the way the human body worked, I was inspired to learn more. It was all so elegantly complicated yet could be dissected into little discoveries to chip away at the mystery. I wanted to add another piece to the puzzle. Anyone in science knows that it is very rare that you make a big discovery. What is more common is that you uncover a small building block that eventually helps someone else make a big breakthrough.

Daily Practice

Mantra

"I play a small part in something greater than myself."

"I'm not expected to complete the task, but I'm not free to stop trying."

Does it make you feel small to say that mantra out loud? The purpose of this mantra is not to feel small per se but to realize that there is so much that is really big out there. When we start feeling bigger than we are, our humility gets out of balance. We need to remember that there is something greater than us out there that is setting the bar.

The evil inclination feeds us messages that we are bigger than we really are. One way this manifests is a cognitive illusion called the illusion of control, which says that people think they can control outcomes over which they have no power. For example, people playing the dice game craps will throw the dice hard if they need to make a big number and softly if they need to make a small number. How hard you throw the dice doesn't actually affect the outcome, but we suffer from the illusion that our actions can influence this random event.[235] On a spiritual level, this is the evil inclination feeding our ego, a failure to realize how small our role really is.

Observe

American Mussar teaches us everyday, practical spirituality. How do you feel about awe? Does it seem like we've crossed into the woo-woo? If that is the case, it is worth taking some time to explore those feelings. Where do they come from? You've made it this far in the book, and in an age when most people don't read past the first few chapters of a book, which means that something here is working for you. The voice that is casting shade on the idea of "something greater" is the evil inclination, which is trying to undermine the great work you have demonstrated by reading this far. Become the watcher and practice equanimity. Observe the feelings, but don't let them derail your exploration of awe.

Nature, science, music, art, people—all are sources of awe.

How does awe fit into your life? Where do you see awe? Are you in awe of people, making them into idols and the subject of inappropriate worship?

For you, perhaps there is no awe in your life. Nothing is sacred, the world is there for your convenience, and you don't find meaning or inspiration in anything.

---

235 Thompson, "Illusions of Control," in *Cognitive Illusions*, 122.

Watch without judgment, and record what you see in your journal at the first opportunity.

From My Journal

I was down and very unsure of myself this morning—it was hard to look for God. I kept trying to see the infinite because that is the assignment [from the Mussar class] and not connecting but kept trying. Then the sun poked through the clouds, and I lowered the shade in Peets. I could see the sun and clouds through the lattice—I could see patterns everywhere and could sense the infinite. The sun is behind every cloud. I felt better.

There was a sub in yoga, and only three people, but I went with it even though part of me wanted to leave. Was able to perceive the infinite while meditating.

Act

What are some of the things that we can do to practice the awe of majesty? Or, put another way, where do we find something greater than ourselves?

- **Go into nature.** Scientific studies show that as people move out of cities, away from buildings and into the trees, their stress goes down and their immune system function improves.[236] We evolved in a natural environment. Just being out in nature, surrounded by living things, brings a natural sense of peace. We feel at home and can be inspired to take on our next challenge.

- **Look for patterns.** The laws of nature and geometry are both reflections of the way that the Divine created the universe. As I shared in my journal entry, I was able to find the Divine by looking through a mesh shade over a window. As I looked through the shade at the building across the street, the entire structure had become pixelated. I could see in incredible detail

---

236 Phys.org, "Green Environments Essential for Human Health."

where each section of the window started and stopped. Each window had its own set of pixels, and the roof was separated from the sky by a line of pixels. I was in awe.

You can create a similar effect by squinting, closing your eyes so that you can barely see. Look at the patterns that remain. It is almost as if there is an underlying truth or wholeness that comes through in those moments.

- **Say a prayer of thanks.** The twentieth-century Jewish philosopher Rabbi Abraham Joshua Heschel said, "To pray is to take notice of the wonder, to regain a sense of the mystery."[237] The prayer could be a simple thank-you for the latest small wonder you have been given by the universe (or by the Divine, if you prefer).

- **Pray to become unstuck.** Earlier in the chapter I described how too much awe can lead to becoming stuck. We say a simple prayer to help us open our mouths to pray, to overcome the fear of being in the presence of the Divine. When you become stuck, such that you know what you should do but are feeling stuck and can't actually do it, say a prayer for help. Close your eyes, take a deep breath, and focus your attention on your request. "Please help me find the strength to_____." This simple prayer will help you move forward.

Okay, this may seem hokey, and I suspect that some of you are skeptical. If that is the case, let me ask you, have you ever tried it? Are you absolutely sure that it will do no good to say a short prayer? Maybe you are afraid of what it would mean if it does help. Even if praying does help you become unstuck, let me reassure you it does not mean that you will need to accept that the supernatural was involved, nor will you be required to become a believer if you are not one today. It may be that

---

237 Heschel, *The Wisdom of Heschel*, 208.

for purely psychological reasons a moment of focus and slower breathing can help you move forward.

However, I must emphasize that the "asking for help" part is important. I can sense another reaction from some of you, who may be thinking, "But I don't like asking for help." Interesting, isn't it? No one of us can get through this world alone. Asking the Unseen for help may help you get through your mental block about asking for human assistance. What soul trait is keeping you from asking for help? Write about it in your journal.

• **Sing.** Rabbi Nachman of Breslov said, "The most direct way to attach ourselves to God in this material world is through music and song. Even if you can't sing well, sing. Sing to yourself. Sing in the privacy of your home. But sing." If you are unsure of Divinity, think of this as attaching yourself to something greater.

Conclusion

◆

Continue Taking Action

Assumption: We All Carry a Divine Spark That Is Occluded By Our Baggage

I taught my first Mussar class on the afternoon of Yom Kippur. Late in the morning I had a powerful dream while in services; some say it was a vision.

I was outside at night, and someone said that the stars had all disappeared. I looked up into the sky and all I could see was black. There were no stars anywhere to be seen.

I turned to the left, looked over my shoulder, and saw a giant, flaming rectangle in the sky. It was up in the heavens, and it was like this flame had been moving across the sky, devouring all of the stars. I then looked back to where the sky was empty and looked more closely. Now I could see that the stars were not completely gone. I could see tiny little halos, almost like a corona, where each star had been. I could see the little coronas for all of the stars.

I thought to myself, this is like the divine spark in everyone that occludes our baggage. If we look hard enough, we can still see a little bit of that divine spark no matter what is in the way.

Conclusion

Now take a moment and look back over your practice. You've completed reading about the thirteen soul traits I've included in this book. Take a moment to reflect.

Have you taken any action?

Do you feel any different?

Were there times when you surprised yourself by responding to a challenge in an unusually balanced way?

What challenges have you experienced?

What challenges remain?

If you haven't taken any action and don't notice anything different, don't despair! Just by finishing this book you've taken an action, and you have an opportunity to continue on to the next step. Since you've come this far, you are the kind of person who wants to make changes. It is okay if you haven't noticed any changes because you have changed. You won't see the change until the right choice point comes up. In fact, you have a choice right now: will you stop or will you continue on to the next step?

One of my students took my Mussar class the first three years I offered it. He loved the community and the discussion. He bought *Everyday Holiness* and would urge others to read it, although he didn't read it much himself. At the end of the year he felt happy that so many others found their lives had changed, yet he still felt the same. Finally, he asked, "This is just an intellectual exercise, isn't it?" He began to realize the practical applications of Mussar and wished he had done more.

The second year was similar to the first. In the last class, he said that he felt bad because he hardly did anything outside of class and once again felt that he had not changed that much at all. He asked me if that was okay. I thought long and hard before answering.

The first thought that came to mind was "you get out what you put in." But that answer carries a blaming/shaming vibe, which is neither kind nor helpful. I thought some more. It wasn't like he was putting in nothing. All along, he was contributing to the class—a lot. He was super busy, yet he found time and made it a priority to come to class regularly. In fact, he attended more classes than anyone else. I realized that because he made time to be with us every class, his soul must be crying out for change. Here is how I answered: "We are only expected to take that next step on our journey. For you, that step was coming to class each week and not giving up. Your work has been making changes in your soul—they are just too small to see."

In the fall he returned for the third year, and things were different. He started reading the chapters in the book and on occasion wrote long, heartfelt passages in his journal. His comments in class were different. For the first time, he started to admit some painful truths about himself. His whole demeanor began to change, and he started to have a more self-confident air. And outside of class he is participating and enjoying our community so much more. He continues on his journey as I write this.

Another student took the class for a year and part of another, and then did not return. During her time as a student she often shared how she felt more patient and more at peace. I ran into her a year after she stopped coming. She laughed as she said that she was regressing.

Rabbi Eliyahu Dessler, who wrote his Mussar masterpiece *Strive for Truth* in England in the early twentieth century, taught that the evil inclination is patient and sometimes operates by telling us we are done. Rabbi Dessler writes, "The Joy of victory [over the evil inclination] becomes the weapon" as complacency sets in, and the evil inclination can attack again.[238] Not only is it possible that this will happen to you, it is likely to. This is but a more advanced kind of test.

The Great Wall of Mussar

The first few months of Mussar practice are often great. We are excited as we see ourselves moving toward balance. Soon we may begin to see Mussar connections everywhere and feel like we have it all figured out. Then one day we do something really boneheaded from a Mussar perspective. Progress seems to stop as we realize that for all we've

---

238 Dessler, *Strive for Truth,* 46.

done, we remain broken, and we start to feel like giving up. When this happens to you, rejoice because it means that you are making real progress!

I call it the Great Wall of Mussar, aka the Revenge of the Evil Inclination. As we are making progress by strengthening the good inclination, the evil inclination is biding its time, quietly getting stronger too. It is waiting for a moment of weakness, a slip, and then it comes pouring out as rage, despair, or a little voice whispering, "See, I told you it was all useless." The Talmud teaches, "The greater the man, the greater his evil inclination."[239]

As you become more balanced, your evil inclination will get stronger too. Expect it, respect it when it comes, and keep going. It will quiet down again soon. In addition, remember how important the evil inclination is in a normal life. It is the source of ambition, drive, and will. While the EI is getting stronger, your ability to control and channel it in positive directions will get stronger too.

The only graduation from your spiritual curriculum is death. I'm in no hurry to get there. In life, we can't expect to one day find enlightenment, move on to a higher plane, and somehow become better than others. When we start to think those thoughts, it is time to go back to the beginning, to the study of humility. "No more than my space, no less than my place" is a mantra that will serve you well.

What Is It That You Seek?

What is it that you seek? We live in a world that bombards us with marketing, telling us everything we lack so that we may seek salvation in material things. The workplace asks for our unrivaled devotion, and the pace of life in an always-on world of 24/7 connection is exhausting. But things are starting to change. There is a quiet counterculture that is starting to do things differently.

While the technology today is different, your fundamental human choices are the same as they have always been. Do you focus on your-

---

239 Sukkah 52a.

self or do you focus on other people? Is the answer in the material or is it in the spiritual? Do you need something else or do you already have everything you need?

The collective wisdom of our Jewish ancestors is there to help us when our hearts are open to change. King David asked for the following in Psalm 27:

> Just one thing have I asked of the Lord;
> only this will I seek:
> to live in the house of the Lord
> all the days of my life.[240]

What does King David mean? I think he is saying, "I want to live a good life and be a good person." Living in "the house of the Lord" is a way of living an ethical life, one that is open to people of any creed or faith and to believers and non-believers alike. The doors were always open to King David, despite his many flaws, and the doors remain open for us as well.

The door is in front of us multiple times every day: we can choose to go in or remain outside.

The door is in front of you right now. What will you do?

---

240 Psalm 27:4.

Acknowledgments

◆

They say writing is a lonely endeavor, which was certainly the case for my first book. For this book, however, I almost never felt alone, which I directly credit to Mussar. In fact, this book is a step on my personal Mussar journey, and I would be remiss if I did not thank those people who helped me get started.

I owe a great debt to Rabbi Jennifer Clayman, who first introduced me to Mussar, and to Rabbi Sarah Weissman, who both supported my desire to teach Mussar at Congregation Beth Am and helped made it happen. I am also indebted to Emily Osterman, who managed the calendaring; Liz Vaisben, who helped get the word out; and executive director Rachel Tasch for support and friendship in ways both large and small. To round out the Beth Am thanks, I would be remiss if I didn't thank Rabbi Janet Marder for her kind and insightful feedback on the introduction. You should thank her too, since I deleted four very mediocre pages based on the issues she raised.

Special thanks to my Mussar teacher Alan Morinis for his continuous insights, writing, leadership, and encouragement. Alan, you are a spark among sparks. Thank you also to the wonderful participants at the 2014 Mussar Institute Kallah (retreat), which was absolutely life-changing for me. I arrived with a rough manuscript and a desire to eventually get a book out while continuing to grow my coaching business, and I left with laserlike focus on devoting my life to Mussar. Two months later I had book proposal and an agent, and a month after that I had a publisher.

On the writing side, thanks to Steve and Bill Harrison, whose Quantum Leap Coaching Program and individual coaching helped prepare me to write and market a successful book. Particular shout-out to a few Quantum Leap coaches: Geoffrey Berwind for teaching me the art of storytelling, Martha Bullen for advice on writing and publishing, Mary Giuseffi on personal branding, and Debra W. Englander for her help on the book proposal. Fellow Quantum Leaper Letha Marchetti has been an amazing friend and accountability partner. Thank you, Letha, for your support, encouragement, and suggestions every day at 8:30 AM. Most importantly, Quantum Leap introduced me to my wonderful agent, Jeff Herman. Jeff, thanks so much for tirelessly shopping the book proposal until it found a great home at Llewellyn, and for your continuing advice and support.

And thank you to the amazing Llewellyn team, including Angela Wix, Becky Zins, Kat Sanborn, Alisha Bjorklund, Kevin Brown, Tom Lund, and Anna Levine.

Quantum Leap also gave me access to Ann McIndoo's writing program, which helped me organize the materials and write a first draft in just ninety days. Special thanks to my writing coach Mishael Patton and Katie Rogers, who transcribed hours of the "talked" first draft.

A book can't exist without readers, and readers just came out of the woodwork to help me find the good and bad as *The Spiritual Practice of Good Actions* took shape. This included longtime writing friends like Jarie Bolander, Tracy Shawn, and Dianne Olberg, as well as some new readers from the Mussar community, namely Jerry Schermer and Joanie Zecherle. And thank you to my friend Debby Satten for some timely feedback with short notice. Thank you all; your comments and encouragement were invaluable. Jerry was also my Mussar study partner during the bulk of the writing, and his companionship on the journey was a light and an inspiration.

Acknowledgments

Two readers get mentioned for heroic reading above and beyond the call of duty. Their efforts can only be classified as loving-kindness because they so selflessly helped me build the book.

Nancy Weiss, who leads a wonderful Mussar group that I am a part of, spent hours reading, rewording, and discussing the book with me on the phone. Thank you, dear friend.

Barbara Gottesman is new to Mussar, and seemingly out of nowhere arrived in my life and completely reworked the five chapters of the book. My apologies to the readers who had to endure the first versions of these chapters without Barb's wonderful feedback.

Some special mentions:

- Shira Dicker, my extraordinary Jewish-community publicist

- Jennifer McCabe and Lynne Dartnall for administrative help

- Stephanie Brandt for allowing me to use her wonderful photo of the confluence of the Arv and Rhone rivers

- Jason Eversman and Katie Carroll for formatting the notes

- Felicia Clark, whose expertise on body image helped me bring the teaching that "the bride is always beautiful" into the twenty-first century

- Current and former Mussar students for everything you have taught me

- Every barista within ten miles of San Carlos for your decaffeinated soy beverages

- The angel contributors for the Pocket Mensch app, including Adam Frankl in memory of Stella Frankl, Marie Kindt, and Larry Rosenberg

Finally, I could not be living my dream without the love and support of my wife, Rachel, and my daughters. I love you all.

Appendix I

♦

Mussar Overview

Mussar consists of daily, weekly, and yearly practice cycles.

Daily Practice

As part of your daily Mussar practice, each morning you will get up and review the mantra for whatever soul trait you are presently studying. If you are studying trust, your mantra is "trust in God but tie your camel." As you proceed throughout the day, be mindful of how trust is affecting your decisions. In the evening before you go to bed, open your journal and write a few words describing how trust came into play during the day. Whether you were happy with what you did or wish you had done things differently, it doesn't matter: just write about it.

Just this act of reviewing and remembering these traits will start to make changes in your subconscious. It will make changes in your soul. You may not feel them now, but someday, suddenly, something will happen, and you will be amazed that you handled it in a completely different way.

The mantras for the thirteen soul traits covered in this book are:

Humility: *Occupy a rightful space, neither too much nor too little*

Patience: *This too shall pass, and I have the strength to get by until it does*

Enthusiasm: *Make the most of each moment*

Trust: *Trust in God but tie your camel*

Loving-Kindness: *Sustain others without the thought of reward, even if they don't deserve it*

Truth: *Be distant from falsehood*

Honor: *Find the good in anyone*

Gratitude: *Give thanks for the good and the bad*

Order: *First things first and last things later*

Silence: *Nothing is better than silence*

Equanimity: *Better to surf the waves of life than get pounded or swept away*

Fear of Consequences: *Fear consequences but not action*

Awe of Majesty: *I play a small part in something greater than myself*

Weekly Practice

Spend two weeks on each trait. At the end of each week, take a few minutes to reread your journal. Do you notice anything about the ebb and flow? Mussar is not a linear practice. Yes, we want to take the next step, but sometimes we will take backward steps; sometimes we take big steps backward. That is okay; we are human and imperfect. This is to be expected.

Even if you feel like you are not making progress, rest assured that you are making progress. Those small changes are building up within your soul. I will say that if Mussar practice never takes you out of your comfort zone—if you are not doing anything differently in any way—then maybe you are not trying hard enough.

Maybe you need to have a bit more courage. Maybe your fear of consequences is out of balance and you need to practice doing something that is a little bit courageous, like going on a roller coaster or leaving work just a few minutes early or having lunch in the cafeteria instead of at your desk. You need to start taking steps to move beyond your comfort zone.

At the end of twenty-six weeks, return to the first trait and begin practicing it again. These thirteen steps offer a cycle where each trait is practiced for four weeks.

Yearly Practice

We have an opportunity to practice Mussar until the end of our days. On Yom Kippur we are taught to live each day as if it may be your last because it could be your last. In addition to the daily and weekly practice, I suggest a yearly practice.

The first is a yearly life inventory, and Yom Kippur is a perfect time to conduct it. If you haven't observed Yom Kippur in the past, try taking the day off next year. Yom Kippur usually falls in September, one of the busiest months of the year. Take a leap of faith and unplug from your life for a day. Look for a community to share the day with. Think about where you are and what you would like to do differently.

Do you have unused vacation days? Are you one of these people who has months of vacation time because you are too busy working? What soul trait is governing this imbalance in your life? Is it fear? Is it humility? It is time to schedule a vacation.

Make It Easy for Yourself

Mussar is a wonderful practice that will change your life. Yisroel Salanter and his disciples created the Mussar movement of the nineteenth century by innovation. My website, americanmussar.com, is my attempt to bring you innovative products to help your practice in the twenty-first century. You are invited to visit americanmussar.com to find free tools, products, and community to support your practice.

Appendix II

◆

English to Hebrew Terms

Awe of Majesty: *Yirah*

Choice Point: *Bechirah* Point

Divine Presence: *Shechinah*

Enthusiasm: *Zerizut,* which is also translated into English as "alacrity"

Equanimity: *Menuchat Ha'nefesh* (calmness of the soul)

Evil Inclination: *Yetzer hara*

Fear of Consequences: *Yirah*

Good Deed: derives from the Hebrew word *mitzvah,* which is more accurately translated to English as "a commandment from God"

Good Inclination: *Yetzer hatov*

Gratitude: *Hakarat hatov* (recognizing the good)

Appendix II

Honor: *Kavod*

Humility: *Anavah*

Loving-Kindness: *Chesed*

Mussar Group: *Va'ad*

Order: *Seder*

Patience: *Savlanut*

Rabbi: *Reb, Rebbeinu, R. Rav, Rebbi*

Righteous: *Tzaddikim*

Silence: *Sh'tikah*

Study Partner: *Chevrutah*

Trust: *Bitachon*

Truth: *Emet*

Bibliography

Books

Alcoholics Anonymous: The Big Book, 4th ed. New York: Alcoholics Anonymous World Services, 2001.

Bialik, Hayyim Nahman, and Yehoshua Hana Ravnitzky, eds. *The Book of Legends (Sefer Ha-Aggadah): Legends from the Talmud and Midrash*, trans. William G. Braude. New York: Schocken, 1992.

Brown, Brené. *Daring Greatly*. New York: Penguin, 2012.

Buber, Martin. *Tales of the Hasidim, Book 1: The Early Masters,* trans. Olga Marx. New York: Schocken, 1991.

Dessler, Rabbi Eliyahu E. *Strive for Truth!* trans. Aryeh Carmell. Jerusalem: Feldheim, 1978.

Diamant, Anita. *Pitching My Tent*. New York: Scribner, 2005.

Falk, Marcia. *The Book of Blessings*. San Francisco: Harper, 1996.

Gaon, Sadia. *The Book of Beliefs and Opinions*. New Haven: Yale University, 1989.

Bibliography

Glick, Rabbi Yoel. *Living the Life of Jewish Meditation: A Comprehensive Guide to Practice and Experience.* Woodstock, VT: Jewish Lights, 2014.

Gold, Shefa. *Torah Journeys: The Inner Path to the Promised Land.* Teaneck, NJ: Ben Yehuda Press, 2006.

Goleman, Daniel. *A Force for Good: The Dalai Lama's Vision for Our World.* New York: Bantam, 2015.

Green, Arthur. *Judaism's 10 Best Ideas: A Brief Guide for Seekers.* Woodstock, VT: Jewish Lights, 2014.

Haidt, Jonathan. *The Happiness Hypothesis: Finding Modern Truth in Ancient Wisdom.* New York: Basic, 2006.

Heschel, Abraham Joshua, and Ruth M. Goodhill. *The Wisdom of Heschel.* New York: MacMillan, 1986.

Hockenbury, Don H., and Sandra E. Hockenbury. *Psychology.* New York: MacMillan, 2005.

Hough, Karen. *The Improvisation Edge: Secrets to Building Trust and Radical Collaboration at Work.* San Francisco: Berrett-Koehler, 2011.

ibn Paquda, Rabbi Bachya. *Duties of the Heart,* Hebrew trans. Rabbi Yehuda ibn Tibbon Feldheim, English trans. Daniel Haberman. Jerusalem: Feldheim, 1996.

JPS Hebrew-English Tanakh: The Traditional Hebrew Text and the New JPS Translation. Philadelphia: Jewish Publication Society, 1999.

Kushner, Harold S. *Overcoming Life's Disappointments.* New York: Random House, 2006.

Levin, Menahem Mendel. *Cheshbon HaNefesh (Accounting of the Soul).* Jerusalem: Feldheim, 1995.

Lew, Alan. *This Is Real and You Are Completely Unprepared: The Days of Awe as a Journey of Transformation.* Boston: Little, Brown, 2003.

Luzzatto, Moshe Hayyim. *Path of the Just,* trans. Yosef Liebler. Jerusalem: Feldheim, 2004.

———. *Mesillat Yesharim: The Path of the Upright*, trans. Mordechai Kaplan; introduction and commentary by Ira F. Stone. Philadelphia, PA: Jewish Publication Society, 2010.

Marcus, Greg. *Busting Your Corporate Idol: Self-help for the Chronically Overworked*. San Carlos, CA: Idolbuster Coaching Institute, 2014.

Mogel, Wendy. *The Blessing of a B Minus: Using Jewish Teachings to Raise Resilient Teenagers*. New York: Scribner, 2011.

Morinis, Alan. *Every Day, Holy Day: 365 Days of Teachings and Practices from the Jewish Tradition of Mussar*. Boston: Trumpeter, 2010.

———. *Everyday Holiness: The Jewish Spiritual Path of Mussar*. Boston: Trumpeter, 2007.

———. *With Heart in Mind: Mussar Teachings to Transform Your Life*. Boston: Trumpeter, 2014.

Pirkei Avos Treasury: The Sages Guide to Living with an Anthologized Commentary & Anecdotes. Edited by Nosson Scherman with commentary by Moshe Lieber. New York: Mesorah, 1995.

Putnam, Robert D. *Bowling Alone: The Collapse and Revival of American Community*. New York: Touchstone, 2000.

Riso, Don Richard, and Russ Hudson. *The Wisdom of the Enneagram*. New York: Bantam, 1999.

Steinschneider, Moritz. *The Hebrew Translations of the Middle Ages and the Jews as Transmitters, Vol. I*. New York, London: Springer, 2013.

Stone, Ira F. *A Responsible Life: The Spiritual Path of Mussar*. Kindle edition. New York: Aviv Press, 2013.

Telushkin, Rabbi Joseph. *Words That Hurt, Words That Heal: How to Choose Words Wisely and Well*. New York: William Morrow, 1998.

Thompson, Suzanne C. "Illusions of Control," in Rudiger Pohl, ed., *Cognitive Illusions: A Handbook on Fallacies and Biases in*

Thinking, Judgment and Memory. New York: Psychology Press, 2004.

Tolle, Eckhart. *The Power of Now: A Guide to Spiritual Enlightenment.* Novato, CA: New World Library, 1999.

Umansky, Ellen M., and Dianne Ashton, eds. *Four Centuries of Jewish Women's Spirituality: A Sourcebook.* Boston: Beacon Press, 1992.

Zaloshinsky, Rabbi Gavriel, ed. *The Ways of the Tzaddikim: Orchot Tzaddikim,* trans. Rabbi Shraga Silverstein. Jerusalem: Feldheim, 1994.

Periodicals

Firozi, Paulina. "378 People 'Pay It Forward' at Starbucks," *USA Today,* August 21, 2014.

Kershner, Isabel. "Israeli Girl, 8, at Center of Tension over Religious Extremism," *New York Times,* December 27, 2011.

Koerner, Allyson. "'Dancing with the Stars' Robert Herjavec Explains Honoring His Late Mother through Dance in Touching Essay," *Bustle,* April 7, 2015.

Kristof, Nicholas D. "Tokyo Journal: When Doctor Won't Tell Cancer Patient the Truth," *New York Times,* February 25, 1995.

Morinis, Alan. "The Middot Perspective: The Spiritual Elevation of Everyday Choices," *Jewish Spirituality,* 2004.

Safire, William. "On Language; The Elision Fields," *New York Times,* August 13, 1989.

Tierney, John. "A Serving of Gratitude May Save the Day," *New York Times,* November 21, 2011.

Web

Afsai, Shai. "Benjamin Franklin, Mussar Maven," Forward.com, January 17, 2011, http://forward.com/opinion/134721 /benjamin-franklin-mussar-maven/.

Bibliography

American Psychological Association, "Stress Weakens the Immune System," http://www.apa.org/research/action/immune.aspx.

"The Amygdala & Emotions," Effective Mind Control, http://www.effective-mind-control.com/amygdala.html.

"Ancient Jewish History: The Great Revolt," Jewish Virtual Library, https://www.jewishvirtuallibrary.org/jsource/Judaism/revolt.html.

Angvall, Elizabeth. "Stress! Don't Let It Make You Sick," AARP Bulletin, November 2014, http://www.aarp.org/health/healthy-living/info-2014/stress-and-disease.html.

Apple, Raymond. "Know Before Whom You Stand," *Ask the Rabbi* (blog), http://www.oztorah.com/2007/06/know-before-whom-you-stand-ask-the-rabbi.

Babylonian Talmud, http://www.come-and-hear.com/tcontents.html.

Brombacher, Shoshannah. "A Pillow Full of Feathers," Chabad.org, http://www.chabad.org/library/article_cdo/aid/812861/jewish/A-Pillow-Full-of-Feathers.htm.

Busch, Andrew E. "The New Deal Comes to a Screeching Halt in 1938," The Ashbrook Center, Ashland University, May 2006, http://ashbrook.org/publications/oped-busch-06-1938.

Cesarani, David. "Nicholas Winton Saved Jewish Children, But He Also Has a Lesson for Our Current Migrant Crisis," *The Guardian*, July 5, 2015, http://www.theguardian.com/commentisfree/2015/jul/05/nicholas-winton-refugee-crisis-hero-whitehall-immigration.

Chyet, Stanley F. "The Political Rights of the Jews in the United States: 1776–1840," http://americanjewisharchives.org/publications/journal/PDF/1958_10_01_00_chyet.pdf.

The Complete Jewish Bible with Rashi Commentary, http://www.chabad.org/library/bible_cdo/aid/63255/jewish/The-Bible-with-Rashi.htm.

Emmons, Robert. "Why Gratitude Is Good," Greater Good, http://greatergood.berkeley.edu/article/item/why_gratitude_is_good/.

Glick, Rabbi Yoel. "Mediations By Teacher," Winter Feast for the Soul, http://winterfeastforthesoul.com/index2.php?dest=meditations_glick.

Jewish Spirituality: The Magazine, http://www.jspirituality.org/middot1.html.

Levin, Dan. "Dust and Ashes—and Holy," ReformJudaism.org, http://www.reformjudaism.org/dust-and-ashes-and-holy#sthash.SR2S79sm.dpuf.

Living Life Fully, http://www.livinglifefully.com/wonder.htm.

L'Neshama, Revach. "Rav Yisroel Salanter's Expensive Cup of Coffee," http://revach.net/stories/mashal/Rav-Yisroel-Salanters-Expensive-Cup-of-Coffee/4564.

Luzzatto, *Path of the Just*, Shechem.org, http://www.shechem.org/torah/mesyesh.

Maderer, Rabbi Jill. "Turning Fate Into Destiny with A Shabbat Lie," *BlogRS*, October 31, 2016, https://rodephshalom.wordpress.com/2015/10/31/turning-fate-into-destiny-with-a-sabbath-lie/.

Marder, Rabbi Janet. "The Call: Erev Rosh Hashana 5773," a sermon on the night of Rosh Hashanah, September 16, 2012, quoting Chaim David HaLevy, former Sephardic Chief Rabbi of Israel, Aseh L'cha Rav, 2:64; *Work, Workers and the Jewish Owner*, http://www.betham.org/sermon/call-erev-rosh-hashana-5773.

McFadden, Robert D. "Nicholas Winton, Rescuer of 669 Children from Holocaust, Dies at 106," *New York Times*, July 1,

2015, http://www.nytimes.com/2015/07/02/world/europe
/nicholas-winton-is-dead-at-106-saved-children-from-the
-holocaust.html.

National Public Radio, "Brain Maturity Extends Well Beyond
Teen Years," October 10, 2011, http://www.npr.org
/templates/story/story.php?storyId=141164708.

New International Version of the Bible, Biblica, http://www
.biblica.com/en-us/the-niv-bible/.

Oxford Dictionaries: US English, s.v. "truth," http://www
.oxforddictionaries.com/us/definition/american_english
/truth.

Parshablog, "Is חָמָא רָקָם a hendiadys?" December 14, 2010,
http://parsha.blogspot.com/2010/12/is-%D7%97%D7%A1%
D7%93-%D7%95%D7%90%D7%9E%D7%AA-hendiadys
.html.

Pashman, Susan. "My Big Sabbath Lie—and the Joy It Brought,"
The Forward, October 23, 2015, http://forward.com
/culture/323029/more-than-jews-kept-the-sabbath
/#ixzz3rlp0klOr.

Pederson, Traci. "Meditation Shown to Alter Gray Matter in
Brain," Psych Central, http://psychcentral.com/news
/2015/01/24/meditation-shown-to-alter-gray-matter
-in-brain/80342.html.

Pew Research Center, "A Portrait of Jewish Americans,"
October 1, 2013, http://www.pewforum.org/2013/10/01
/jewish-american-beliefs-attitudes-culture-survey.

Phys.org, "Green Environments Essential for Human Health,"
April 19, 2011, http://phys.org/news/2011-04-green
-environments-essential-human-health.html.

Pirkei Avot (*Ethics of the Fathers*), http://www.chabad.org/library
/article_cdo/aid/680274/jewish/Ethics-of-the-Fathers-Pirkei
-Avot.htm.

Bibliography

Pliskin, Zelig. "Peace of Mind," *Daily Lift* (blog), http://www
.aish.com/sp/dl/46125622.html.

Rogers, Fred. "Tragic Events," The Fred Rogers Company,
http://www.fredrogers.org/parents/special-challenges
/tragic-events.php.

Roosevelt, Franklin D. "Address at Madison Square Garden,
New York City, October 31, 1936," The American Presidency
Project, University of California–Santa Barbara, http://www
.presidency.ucsb.edu/ws/?pid=15219.

Shurpin, Yehuda. "Can Angels Sin?," Chabad.org, http://www
.chabad.org/library/article_cdo/aid/1055341/jewish/Can
-Angels-Sin.htm.

Svenson, Ola. "Are We All Less Risky and More Skillful
Than Our Fellow Drivers?" (PDF), *Acta Psychologica* 47 (2):
143–148. doi:10.1016/0001-6918(81)90005-6.

Tikkun Middot Project, "Facilitators Guide: Savlanut
/Forebearance, Patience," http://tikkunmiddotproject
.wikispaces.com/file/view/7+Savlanut+session.pdf.

Yonah of Gerona, *Gates of Repentance*, trans. Rabbi Yaakov
Feldman; Project Genesis Torah.org., http://www.torah.org
/learning/spiritual-excellence/classes/gor3-9.html.

Index

Index

Enthusiasm, 25–29, 73, 77–80, 82–87, 95, 181, 196, 203, 204, 226, 229

Equanimity, 25–29, 169, 173, 175–185, 196, 204, 210, 226, 229

Evil Inclination, 34–36, 42–44, 47, 55, 60, 71, 78–80, 82, 89–91, 120, 131, 143, 149, 155, 156, 161, 162, 165, 174, 181, 188, 189, 203, 205, 210, 217, 218, 229

Fear of Consequences, 123, 187, 189–192, 194, 195, 226, 227, 229

Franklin, Ben, 10, 56, 234, 238

Free will, 33, 34, 43, 77, 78, 93, 94, 101, 173–175

God, 5, 11, 12, 17, 31, 33, 36, 51, 53, 54, 58, 60, 65, 67–69, 75, 83, 89–94, 96–98, 102, 104, 114, 115, 118, 119, 121, 124, 128, 129, 134, 140, 150, 153, 158, 162–164, 171, 176, 177, 179, 181, 187, 189–191, 194, 198, 199, 202, 206, 207, 211, 213, 225, 226, 229

Good Inclination, 34, 36, 42–44, 89, 90, 143, 156, 161–163, 165, 174, 188, 189, 218, 229

Gratitude, 25–29, 41, 42, 87, 126, 137–140, 142–147, 204, 226, 229, 234, 236

Honor, 1, 10, 25–30, 60, 61, 122, 127–136, 141, 147, 184, 192, 196, 204, 226, 230

Humility, 7, 9, 20, 25–30, 48–57, 59–66, 70–72, 95, 124, 127, 132, 138, 147, 157, 165, 182, 184, 193, 203, 204, 210, 218, 226, 227, 230

Inclination to Evil; *see* Evil Inclination

Inclination to Good; *see* Good Inclination

Index

Kabbalah, 8

Kindness, 29, 37, 102, 107, 108, 110, 113, 116, 120, 121, 125, 138

King David, 83, 162, 219

Love, 2, 8, 41, 59, 67, 71, 86, 104, 106, 110, 121, 165, 197, 200, 207, 208, 223, 251

Loving-Kindness, 25–29, 44, 101–110, 119, 120, 156, 204, 223, 226, 230

Meditation, 38–42, 76, 156, 163, 171, 185, 232, 237, 247, 249

Mogel, Wendy, 72, 75, 233

Morinis, Alan, 6, 8, 9, 17, 32, 44, 49–51, 55, 69, 74, 78, 91, 93, 98, 103, 115, 130, 131, 138, 142, 152, 156, 176, 180, 183, 190, 221, 233, 234

Moses, 53, 54, 56, 57, 140, 153, 191, 199, 202, 206–208

Mussar app (Pocket Mensch), 39, 223

Order, 11, 20, 25–29, 39, 47, 56, 59, 62, 72, 77, 107, 110, 115, 118, 119, 121, 149–159, 164, 179, 184, 188, 193, 203, 204, 226, 230, 246, 248, 250, 252

Parenting, 58, 72, 194

Patience, 7, 20, 21, 25–29, 32, 40, 44, 50, 66, 67, 69–76, 80, 92, 95, 98, 125, 154, 157, 204, 226, 230, 238, 253

Rabbi Abraham Joshua Heschel, 198, 212, 232

Rabbi Abraham Yachnes, 103

Rabbi Akiva, 67

Rabbi Alan Lew, 156, 164, 232

Index

GET MORE AT LLEWELLYN.COM

Visit us online to browse hundreds of our books and decks, plus sign up to receive our e-newsletters and exclusive online offers.

- Free tarot readings • Spell-a-Day • Moon phases
- Recipes, spells, and tips • Blogs • Encyclopedia
- Author interviews, articles, and upcoming events

GET SOCIAL WITH LLEWELLYN

Find us on Facebook

www.Facebook.com/LlewellynBooks

Follow us on

www.Twitter.com/Llewellynbooks

GET BOOKS AT LLEWELLYN

LLEWELLYN ORDERING INFORMATION

Order online: Visit our website at www.llewellyn.com to select your books and place an order on our secure server.

Order by phone:
- Call toll free within the U.S. at 1-877-NEW-WRLD (1-877-639-9753)
- Call toll free within Canada at 1-866-NEW-WRLD (1-866-639-9753)
- We accept VISA, MasterCard, American Express and Discover

Order by mail:
Send the full price of your order (MN residents add 6.875% sales tax) in U.S. funds, plus postage and handling to: Llewellyn Worldwide, 2143 Wooddale Drive Woodbury, MN 55125-2989

POSTAGE AND HANDLING

STANDARD (U.S. & Canada):
(Please allow 12 business days)
$30.00 and under, add $4.00.
$30.01 and over, FREE SHIPPING.

INTERNATIONAL ORDERS:
$16.00 for one book, plus $3.00 for each additional book.

Visit us online for more shipping options. Prices subject to change.

FREE CATALOG!

To order, call
1-877-NEW-WRLD
ext. 8236
or visit our website

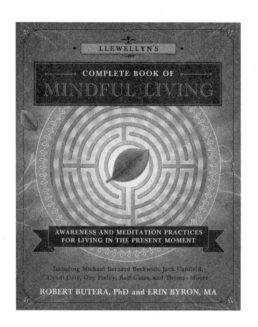

To order, call 1-877-NEW-WRLD

Prices subject to change without notice

Order at Llewellyn.com
24 hours a day, 7 days a week!

Llewellyn's Complete Book
of Mindful Living
Awareness & Meditation Practices
for Living in the Present Moment
Robert Butera, PhD, and Erin Byron, MA

Enhance your awareness, achieve higher focus and happiness, and improve all levels of your health with the supportive practices in this guide to mindful living. Featuring over twenty-five leading meditation and mindfulness experts, *Llewellyn's Complete Book of Mindful Living* shows you how to boost your well-being and overcome obstacles.

With an impressive array of topics by visionary teachers and authors, this comprehensive book provides inspiration, discussion, and specific techniques based on the transformative applications of mindfulness: basic understanding and practices, better health, loving your body, reaching your potential, and connecting to subtle energy and spirit. Using meditation, breathwork, and other powerful exercises, you'll bring the many benefits of mindfulness into your everyday life.

Contributors include Rachel Avalon, Michael Bernard Beckwith, Sarah Bowen, Jeanne Van Bronkhorst, Erin Byron, Robert Butera, Jack Canfield, Alexandra Chauran, Cyndi Dale, Sherrie Dillard, Guy Finley, Rolf Gates, Melissa Grabau, Servet Hasan, Ana Holub, Patricia Johnson, Shakta Khalsa, Melanie Klein, Danielle MacKinnon, Mark A. Michaels, William L. Mikulas, Thomas Moore, Keith Park, Deborah Sandella, Amy B. Scher, Tess Whitehurst, and Angela Wix.

978-0-7387-4677-7
8 x 10 • 384 pp.

THE
ART OF
GOOD
HABITS

Health, Love, Presence & Prosperity

"If you are serious about change and need a roadmap for the process, this book is for you."—Melissa Grabau, PhD, author of *The Yoga of Food*

NATHALIE W. HERRMAN

The Art of Good Habits
Health, Love, Presence & Prosperity
Nathalie W. Herrman

Take ownership of your happiness through simple but effective changes to the way you approach health, love, presence, and prosperity. *The Art of Good Habits* presents a step-by-step action plan to achieve your goals and maintain them for continued success.

Join Nathalie W. Herrman on a life-changing journey toward wellness and satisfaction using this remarkable book as your road map. Gain empowerment and control over life's challenges with effective exercises and easy-to-understand principles. Discover how to look within yourself for answers and change your habits for the better. With this book's four-pillar system—honesty, willingness, awareness, and appreciation—you'll unlock the power of enlightened living.

978-0-7387-4600-5
5 x 7 • 264 pp.

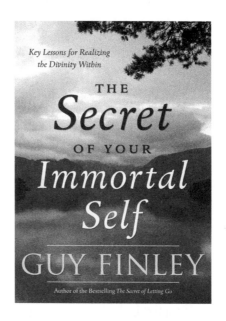

Key Lessons for Realizing
the Divinity Within

THE
Secret
OF YOUR
Immortal
Self

GUY FINLEY

Author of the Bestselling *The Secret of Letting Go*

To order, call 1-877-NEW-WRLD

Prices subject to change without notice

Order at Llewellyn.com
24 hours a day, 7 days a week!

The Secret of Your Immortal Self
Key Lessons for Realizing the Divinity Within

Guy Finley

Open the doors to a new level of self-understanding and let go of useless suffering. *The Secret of Your Immortal Self* helps you seek a deeper, more meaningful relationship with the Divine and provides powerful insights and practical steps on how to find a guiding light in the middle of any dark moment; a light that not only reveals the illusion of imagined self-limitation, but that instantly releases you from the fear of it as well.

Filled with unique and meaningful essays, this guide shows you how to remember a long-forgotten part of your true timeless nature. Piece by piece, this recollection stirs the sleeping soul that, once awakened, guides you to the crowning moment of life: contact with the immortal self. Once achieved, this celestial union releases you from regret, endows you with patience, and grants you the realization that, despite all appearances to the contrary, death is not the end of life.

978-0-7387-4407-0
5 x 7 • 368 pp.

To Write to the Author

If you wish to contact the author or would like more information about this book, please write to the author in care of Llewellyn Worldwide Ltd. and we will forward your request. Both the author and the publisher appreciate hearing from you and learning of your enjoyment of this book and how it has helped you. Llewellyn Worldwide Ltd. cannot guarantee that every letter written to the author can be answered, but all will be forwarded. Please write to:

Greg Marcus
c/o Llewellyn Worldwide
2143 Wooddale Drive
Woodbury, MN 55125-2989

Please enclose a self-addressed stamped envelope for reply or $1.00 to cover costs. If outside the USA, enclose an international postal reply coupon.

Many of Llewellyn's authors have websites with additional information and resources. For more information, please visit our website at

www.llewellyn.com